PROFESSIONAL

SOFT
FURNISHINGS

PROFESSIONAL

SOFT FURNISHINGS

WENDY SHORTER

NEW HOLLAND

First published in 2010 by New Holland Publishers (UK) Ltd
London · Cape Town · Sydney · Auckland

Garfield House
86–88 Edgware Road
London W2 2EA
United Kingdom
www.newhollandpublishers.com

80 McKenzie Street
Cape Town 8001
South Africa

Unit 1
66 Gibbes Street
Chatswood
NSW 2067
Australia

218 Lake Road
Northcote
Auckland
New Zealand

ISBN 978 1 84773 511 9

Senior Editor: Corinne Masciocchi
Photographer: Edward Allwright
Production: Marion Storz
Editorial Direction: Rosemary Wilkinson

2 4 6 8 10 9 7 5 3 1

Reproduction by PDQ Digital Media Solutions Ltd, UK
Printed and bound by Craft Print International Ltd, Singapore

Contents

Introduction	6

GETTING STARTED

Equipment	10
Sundry equipment	13
Sundry materials	14
Curtain and blind sundries	18
Suspension systems	20
Fabrics	22
Measuring and estimating fabrics	38
Sewing techniques	40
Closures	48
Fastenings	50
Passementerie	51
Decorative techniques	54

BASICS

Window treatments

Standard roman blinds	72
Cascade pleated roman blind	76
Roll-up/reef blinds	78

Curtains

Machine-made lined curtains	82
Hand-stitched unlined curtains	84
Hand-stitched lined curtains	85
Interlined curtains	87

Headings

Narrow heading tape with a top frill   89
Pencil pleat tape   91
Puffed heading with tape   92
Encased gathered heading   94
Hand-stitched headings   95

Pleat calculations   96
Pleating patterned fabrics   97
Pleat formations   98
Tab top curtains   104
Eyelet curtains   106
Sheer curtains   108
Tie-backs   109
Piped tie-backs   110
Plaited tie-backs   111
Ruched tie-backs   112
Valances and skirts   113
Yoked valance with spaced box pleats   113
Pelmets   115
Cushions   118

PROJECTS

Lined curtains with a commercial heading tape   124

Tie-backs with contrast piped edge   127

Interlined curtains   129

Roman blind with a contrast panel and beaded trim   133

Bed valance   136

Bed throw   138

Window seat box and bolster cushions   140

Scatter cushions   146

Loose cover for an upright chair   150

Glossary   156
Resources and organizations   157
Acknowledgments and bibliography   158
Index   159

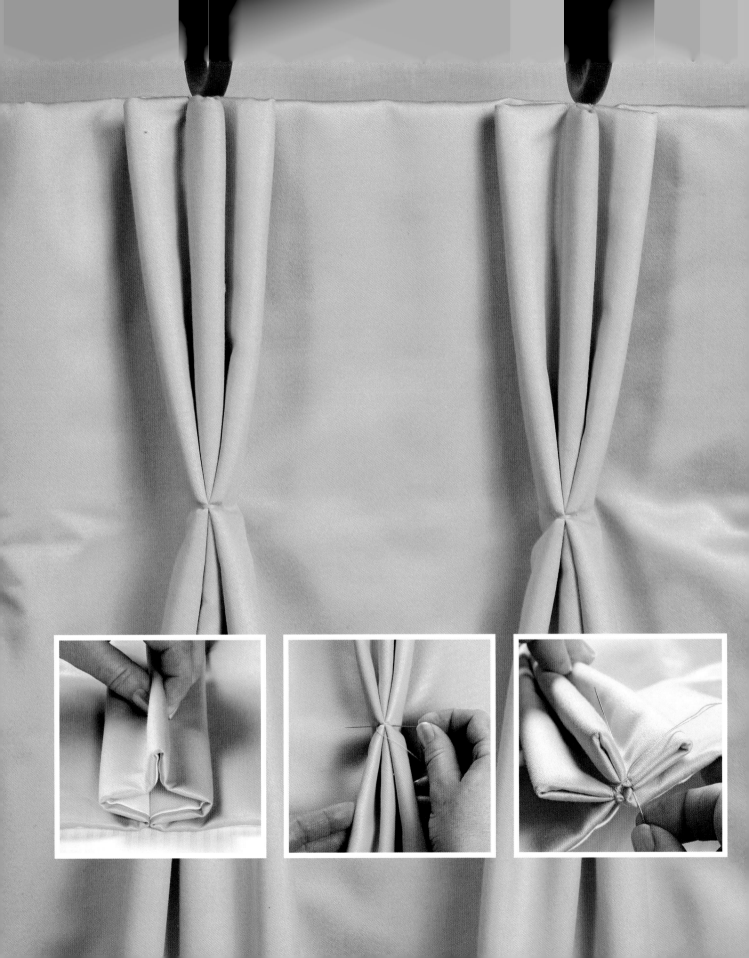

Introduction

I entered the world of professional upholstery and soft furnishings in 1995 after many years working in the film industry as PA to the film director, Stanley Kubrick, and as a freelance Production Co-ordinator.

Having sewn since school, I decided to return to my roots studying at the London Guildhall University, now known as London Metropolitan University and at West Herts College in Hemel Hempstead. I achieved my professional qualifications gaining distinctions for my work, and in 1998 was awarded the Association of Master Upholsterers and Soft Furnishers Student of the Year Award.

Since then I have worked on individual commissions in both upholstery and soft furnishings and was approved for membership of the Association of Master Upholsterers and Soft Furnishers (AMUSF) in 1999. My work has been demonstrated and exhibited at the NEC in Birmingham and the Living Crafts Show at Hatfield House. I am also a visiting lecturer at KLC School of Design at the Chelsea Harbour Design Centre in London. My association with the AMUSF has since lead me to become an active board member and I am currently their Director of Training. I am a Fellow of the AMUSF and in 2009 had the honour of being made a Liveryman of the Worshipful Company of Upholders (the archaic word for upholsterers).

I started my teaching career in 1999 at West Herts College and then back at London Metropolitan University. In July 2006, with the support of some fantastic students, I decided to start my own Training Centre in Hertfordshire. I now run a full range of upholstery and soft furnishings courses for both accredited and leisure courses. The Training Centre has gone from strength to strength, with many of my students achieving credits and distinctions for their work and many have since gone on to start their own very successful businesses.

This book is aimed at those with experience of sewing and soft furnishings who are looking to move onto the next level, or looking to break into the industry. But most importantly, they should have a keen interest in producing good quality decorative furnishings.

I have tried to include as much detail as possible in this book, but nothing can ever take the place of good quality 'hands-on' practical training with a good tutor or practitioner. The projects are based around the training offered at my training centre and will take you through the basics to more complex projects: hand-stitched curtains, decorative detailing, fitted and tailored bedding and loose covers, which I hope will inspire you to create beautiful, professional looking furnishings of your own.

GETTING STARTED

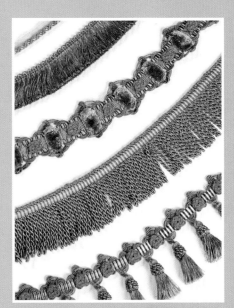

EQUIPMENT

Life as a soft furnisher will be made so much easier with two main pieces of equipment: a cutting table and a sewing machine. There is a large choice of machines available, but don't be dazzled by all the fancy stitches and computerization as you may never need them. Think carefully about your specific needs and choose one that best suits your budget.

WORK BENCH

Like many of my students, my love of soft furnishings started at home with my sewing machine on the dining room table. However, when working on large projects I found it difficult working on my knees on the floor. A bespoke cutting table is very useful but if you can't afford one or don't have the room for one, invest in a 15 mm thick 240 x 120 cm (½ x 8 x 4 in) sheet of MDF (Medium-Density Fibreboard) which can be placed over an existing dining or kitchen table. Cover it in a plastic-coated fabric to protect it. It can then be stored against the wall when not in use and brought out when needed, providing you with a large working surface. If you are fortunate enough to have a designated workroom, then this MDF top can easily be transformed into a workbench with storage underneath for your fabrics and linings.

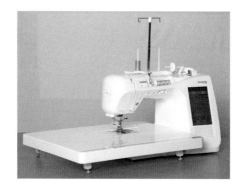

DOMESTIC SEWING MACHINE

Please do not rush out to buy the 'all-singing, all-dancing' expensive sewing machine. As a soft furnisher you won't need one that has hundreds of fancy stitches. What you will need is one that has a good stitch quality, that can take the thickness of fabrics that you may be required to use, and that has a selection of feet you'll find useful.

I recommend a machine that will enable you to lift the presser foot that extra bit higher, in order to take a curtain heading containing lining, interlining and heading buckram, doubled up as it would be for a hand-stitched curtain heading. Always try out the machine before you purchase it, and take along your own samples, as the samples provided tend to be dress-weight fabrics that are too thin and won't give you a realistic idea of the machine's capabilities.

Sewing machine feet

Sewing machines often come with a range of feet and accessories. I prefer a machine that will allow you to use the larger thread spools and that has a good 'walking foot' attachment. A walking foot allows equal pressure on the fabric as it moves under the presser foot and will help alleviate the problem of the fabric slipping, which is particularly important when using silky, shiny fabrics or when you are trying to pattern-match long lengths of fabrics. A walking foot attachment is essential when doing large areas of quilting.

Other useful machine feet are:
- Zip foot that will allow you to stitch close to piping, if the machine does not have a designated piping foot.
- Designated piping foot, if available.
- Concealed zip foot for inserting concealed zips.
- Darning or embroidery foot for free-hand quilting.
- Pin tuck foot.
- Edge foot.

Sewing machine needles

The purpose of the sewing machine needle is to penetrate the fabric, by moving the yarns apart without damaging the fabric. The needle has a long groove on one side, which aids the thread through the yarns, and a small notch, called the scarf, just above the eye of the needle on the other side. This aids the passage of the rotary hook when forming the bottom thread stitch.

Always check that you are using the correct size needle and thread for the fabric you are sewing. The finer the needle, the less damage to the fabric, but if too fine it will blunt and break. Check and change your needle regularly; a blunt needle often causes missed stitching.

Use sharp needles for all woven fabrics and ballpoints for knitted fabrics:

Lightweight fabrics: 70–80 (10–12)
Medium weights: 80–90 (12–14)
Heavy weights: 90–100 (14–16)

MACHINING TIPS

Never push or pull the fabrics through the machine. Instead just guide the fabric, allowing the feed mechanism to take the fabrics through at its own rate. On standard machines, the fabric in contact with the feed mechanism will be taken through faster than the top fabric. This can be a problem when sewing different weights of fabric together. In this case, place the lighter weight fabric underneath and gently apply pressure to this fabric so that both go through at the same rate.

OVERLOCK MACHINE

An overlock machine neatens the raw edges of fabrics, using either a three- or four-thread stitch. This machine is particularly useful when raw edges may be seen or for neatening raw edges on cushion covers. Although not essential – as a good zigzag stitch will suffice – it is a very useful and efficient machine.

INDUSTRIAL MACHINES

Once you start to produce work on a professional basis, you may wish to invest in an industrial sewing machine that is built for continuous use. If you go down this route, take your time and do your research to find a machine that fits your requirements as well as your budget. Although more expensive, I always recommend an alternating compound feed walking foot machine.

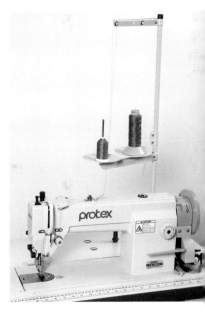

SEWING FAULTS

Here are a number of common faults that can occur when using a sewing machine and their possible causes.

Thread breaks
- Incorrect threading of the machine.
- Thread waste fouling the looper.
- Worn or damaged hole in the throat plate.
- Thread too fine or contains knots.
- Worn or damaged needle.

Needle breaks
- Thread too thick for the needle.
- Operator pulling or pushing the fabric.
- Bobbin case incorrectly fitted.
- Needle is bent.
- Inadequate needle quality.

Irregular seam
- Needle incorrectly fitted.
- Bobbin spool badly wound.
- Bent needle.
- Poor fabric feed.

Poor fabric feed
- Presser foot pressure too low.
- Worn or damaged feed dog.
- Feed dog set too low.
- Inappropriate feeder mechanism.

Missed stitches (the looper does not catch the needle thread):
- Incorrect threading of the machine.
- Incorrect needle or thread.
- Bent needle.
- Incorrect looper settings.

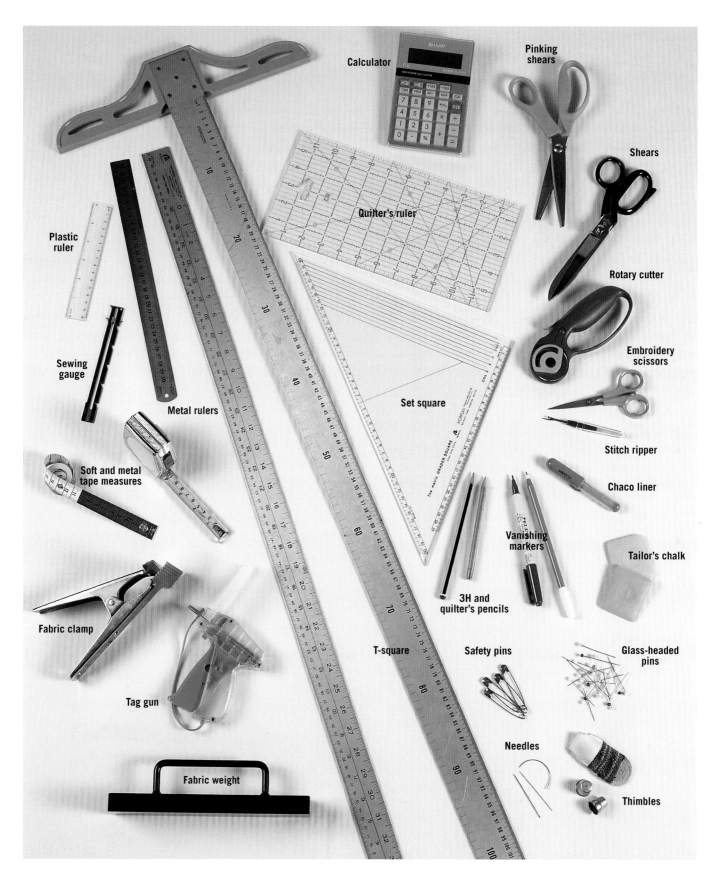

Calculator

Pinking shears

Shears

Quilter's ruler

Rotary cutter

Plastic ruler

Embroidery scissors

Sewing gauge

Metal rulers

Set square

Stitch ripper

Soft and metal tape measures

Chaco liner

Vanishing markers

Tailor's chalk

3H and quilter's pencils

Fabric clamp

T-square

Safety pins

Glass-headed pins

Tag gun

Needles

Fabric weight

Thimbles

SUNDRY EQUIPMENT

There is a huge array of sundry equipment available to the soft furnisher. Some items are a must-have, whereas others look great but are of little use. The following are those I find most useful:

PINS AND NEEDLES

I recommend glass-headed pins about 45 mm (1¾ in) long that are thicker than normal dressmaking pins and can be seen easily, so as not to be left in the fabric by mistake. When pinning fabrics together, pin at right angles to the edge, this way the fabrics are held firmly, avoiding the problem of the fabric slipping or moving.

You will also need a range of sewing needles. I recommend:
- Long darners No.7 (extra long with a large eye).
- Darners No.3 (thicker).
- 2½ in fine curved needles.

TIP Always take pins out as you machine up to them. Although it is possible to machine over them when they are placed at right angles to the edge, you will damage the machine's needle, or even break it, if it hits a pin. This causes damage to the pins and will blunt or break the needle. A blunt needle may cause the sewing machine to miss stitches and may also cause damage to fine fabrics.

SCISSORS

Again, there is a huge array of scissors available, but I recommend:
- Good pair of shears that aren't too heavy and that will only be used for cutting fabrics.
- Short, pointed embroidery scissors.
- Pinking shears.
- Stitch ripper.
- Rotary cutter.

TAPES AND MEASURES

- 5 m (16 ft) or 8 m (26 ft) metal tape measure, preferably with a hook end to aid measuring from the curtain track or pole's suspension point. If you cannot get one with a hook, cut a small piece from each side of the metal end to form a hook that will go through the suspension eye.
- Soft tape measure.
- 15 cm (6 in) and 30 cm (12 in) plastic rulers. These are very useful when measuring and turning in seam allowances as they allow you to crease in the fabric without damaging it.
- Metre stick, preferably 4 cm (1½ in) wide to aid cutting fabrics for piping.
- T-square, preferably 1.5 m (5 ft) long.
- Set square.
- Sewing gauge.

CHALKS AND MARKERS

Always mark fabrics on the wrong side, as markers never really erase well. I prefer to use pencils and a fabric eraser:
- 3H pencil.
- Quilter's pencils.
- Tailor's chalk – always keep a sharp edge on the chalk.
- Chaco liner (in various colours) – very useful as the width of the mark is controlled.
- Water-soluble/vanishing marker pens (be aware, some may vanish too fast!)

THIMBLES

Thimbles are always useful, but I prefer to use soft patchwork thimbles as you have more control in your movements.

Also useful to have in your sewing kit...

- Fabric weights and clamps.
- Calculator.
- Safety pins.
- Tag gun.
- Quilter's ruler.

SUNDRY MATERIALS

Lining, interlining and waddings come in a range of qualities, each designed for a particular purpose. Their aim is to aid the drape and fall of fabrics, particularly fine fabrics and to protect more expensive fabrics from damage by UV light.

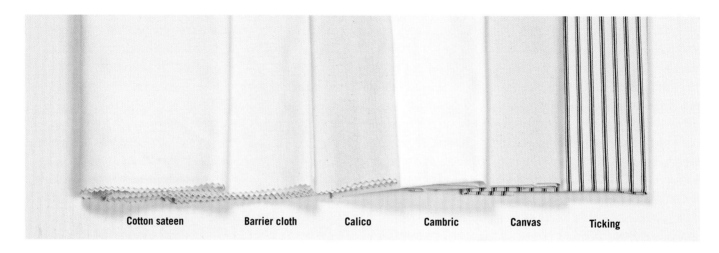

Cotton sateen   Barrier cloth   Calico   Cambric   Canvas   Ticking

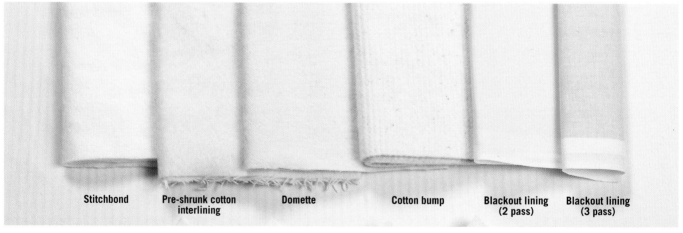

Stitchbond   Pre-shrunk cotton interlining   Domette   Cotton bump   Blackout lining (2 pass)   Blackout lining (3 pass)

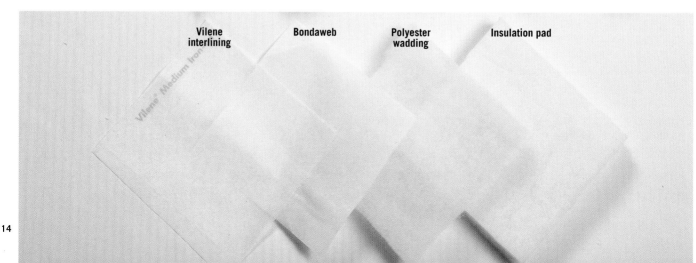

Vilene interlining   Bondaweb   Polyester wadding   Insulation pad

LININGS

It is false economy to buy cheap or coloured lining fabrics. Lining fabric protects expensive fabrics from sun damage and aids the fall and drape of the fabric, so the better the quality, the longer it will last, and the better your curtains will look. They come in a range of colours and qualities. I always use an ivory-coloured lining as any other colour will fade in streaks and will make your curtains look old and tatty before their time. The quality of the lining is determined by the number of 'picks', from standard 96 pick to premium 116 pick.

Cotton sateen. I recommend a good quality 100% cotton sateen sanforized fabric that is crease-resistant and rolled onto a pole rather than lapped (folded in half), as you can never get the crease out.

Barrier cloth is usually a calico- or wool-based cloth that has the required degree of chemical treatment to make it a barrier cloth. When used in conjunction with a covering fabric that contains at least 75% of natural fibres, it will comply with the UK's Furniture & Furnishings (Fire) (Safety) Regulations 1988.

Calico is an inexpensive plain-weave cotton fabric made with carded cotton, which retains small, dark spots normally taken out in more refined cotton fabrics. Available in a range of different weights, with or without fire-retardant treatments.

Cambric is a fine, closely-woven plain-weave fabric of cotton or linen finished with wax, which gives it a slight shine on the wrong side. It is used to make feather cushion cases to help stop the feathers from working through the fabric.

Canvas, sometimes called duck or sail cloth, it is a heavy, coarse, unbleached plain-woven cotton fabric produced in a wide range of weights.

Ticking is a very strong, closely-woven twill cotton fabric, usually woven in narrow black and white stripes and often used to make feather cushion cases, bolsters, pillows and mattresses.

INTERLININGS

When two layers of fabric are used, air is trapped between the layers, increasing the thermal and sound insulation properties, and will create a more pleasing visual effect with more rounded and fuller folds.

Originally, interlinings in curtains were used to help stop the drafts. These days, we use interlinings for their draping qualities and to make thinner fabrics look more sumptuous.

There are various thicknesses and qualities of interlinings. Again, do not buy cheap interlinings as they can be thin and uneven in places, which will not help the hang of your curtains:

Stitchbond is a synthetic (polyester/viscose) interlining that does not shrink and comes in different weights (160–210 grm^2).

Pre-shrunk cotton interlining is a luxurious soft cotton interlining that is pre-shrunk to help avoid future shrinking. Available in a range of weights (260–270 grm^2).

Domette (100% cotton twill) is a thinner, soft cotton interlining ideal for roman blinds, swags and tails, and light-weight curtains. Available in a range of weights (170–265 grm^2).

Cotton bump is a traditional heavy, thick cotton interlining (285 grm^2) with good insulation properties, but it is prone to shrink.

Blackout linings – 2 or 3 pass is used to eliminate light coming through the fabrics. Ideal for use in hotels, for children's rooms or for shift workers. Care must be taken when using blackout linings as pins will leave pinhole marks.

Vilene interlining is a lightweight sew-in or iron-on synthetic stiffening that comes in various thicknesses. Heavier weights are ideal for tie-backs and pelmets.

Bondaweb is a very thin fusible interlining ideal for appliqué.

Lining fabrics can be fire-retardant treated to comply with relevant fire regulations, treated for crease resistance or Teflon®-coated against stains.

WADDINGS

Polyester wadding comes in various weights, from 2½–16 oz.

Insulation pad is polyester wadding on a felted backing. Used in upholstery over serpentine springs, it is also ideal for covering firm pelmet boards.

Polycore 120

Terko satin 36

Decorative threads

Gütermann buttonhole thread

Gütermann polyester thread

Terking Tkt 75

Tre Cerchi

Coats Cotton

Coats Duet

THREADS

Threads are supplied on small reels, spools of 500 metres (546 yd), cross-wound cops and large cones of up to 8000 metres (8750 yd), in various qualities and thicknesses. The higher the number, the thinner the thread. Use a good-quality mercerized cotton thread for hand sewing. Mercerizing is a treatment that makes the thread stronger and more lustrous. Threads should not only match the fabric's colour, but also its weight in order to avoid sewing problems. If you can't find an exact colour match, try one shade darker as it will be less visible than a lighter shade.

Depending on the type of fabrics you are using, you will require a selection of sewing threads for hand stitching, machine sewing and decorative detailing. Some that I find useful are:

- Coats Cotton is a pure mercerized cotton sewing thread.
- Coats Duet is a 100% polyester sewing thread.
- Tre Cerchi is a Tkt 40 thickness mercerized cotton thread that is slightly thicker than the standard dressmaking threads.
- Gütermann thread is a strong polyester thread, but some sewing machines don't work well with polyester threads.

- Terking Tkt 75 is a poly/cotton sewing thread for hand stitching.
- Terko Satin 36 is a good-quality non-mercerized cotton thread that is thicker than the Tre Cerchi and is ideal for sewing in headings on hand-stitched curtains when a stronger thread is required. Gütermann Buttonhole thread is a suitable substitute.
- Polycore 120 is used on overlock machines.
- Embroidery and decorative threads of all kinds can be used for decorative purposes.

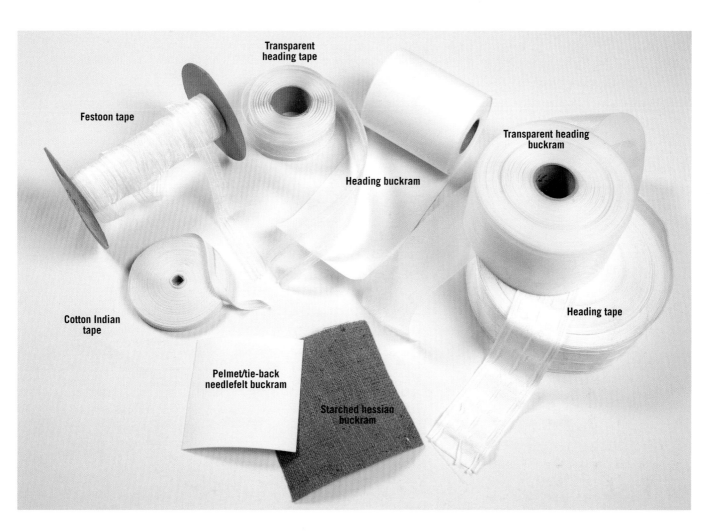

Transparent heading tape

Festoon tape

Transparent heading buckram

Heading buckram

Cotton Indian tape

Heading tape

Pelmet/tie-back needlefelt buckram

Starched hessian buckram

HEADING TAPES AND BUCKRAMS

Your curtains and blinds will need to be hung from the top of the fabrics and most will need firm support to create your chosen headings. There is a wide range of heading tapes and buckrams available, but here is a list of the most useful:

- Heading tapes come pre-strung ready for use in a range of depths and styles. Woven pocket tapes are better than corded pocket tapes as the pockets are less likely to stretch under the weight of the fabrics.
- Transparent heading tapes and heading buckrams are also available for voiles and sheer fabrics.

- Festoon tape is a transparent tape used on the backs of London, Austrian and festoon blinds.
- Heading buckram comes as sew-in or fusible in a range of weights and depths from 10–15 cm (4–6 in).
- Pelmet/tie-back needlefelt buckram.
- Buckram is a stiff finish applied to loose woven cotton or linen used as a stiff interlining. Starched or double-starched hessian is used for larger projects like traditional pelmets, tiebacks and lambrequins.
- Cotton Indian tape is a 13 mm (½ in) wide woven tape.

CURTAIN AND BLIND SUNDRIES

When making curtains and blinds, you will find the following sundry materials useful in aiding the fall of your fabrics and for hanging and fixing finished window treatments in place.

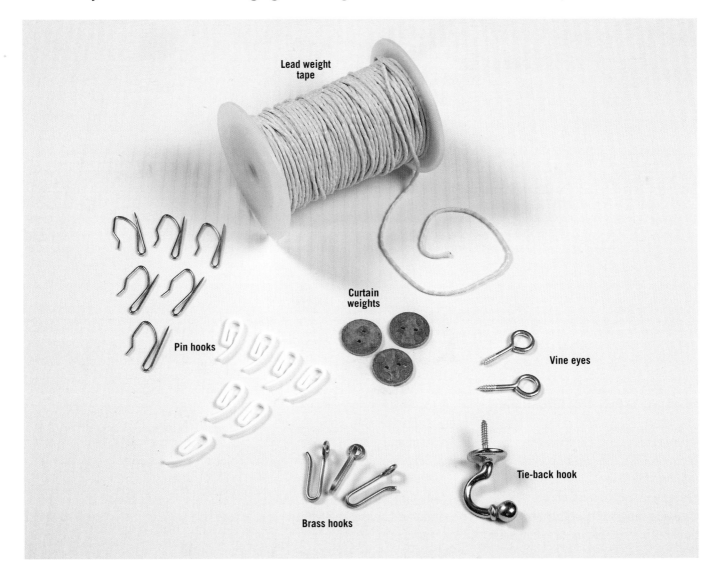

Lead weight tape

Curtain weights

Pin hooks

Vine eyes

Brass hooks

Tie-back hook

CURTAIN SUNDRIES

This is a list of useful curtain sundries that will aid the drape of your curtains.
- Curtain weights are used to weigh down the fabric at seams and the corners of curtains.
- Lead-weighted tape is a small lead chain placed in the hem of voiles and sheer curtains to help weigh them down.
- Pin hooks are for use with hand-stitched heading buckrams.
- Brass hooks are good and strong, but have to be sewn on individually.
- Decorative tie-back hooks.
- Vine eyes are used for securing the end of the curtains or valances to the wall.

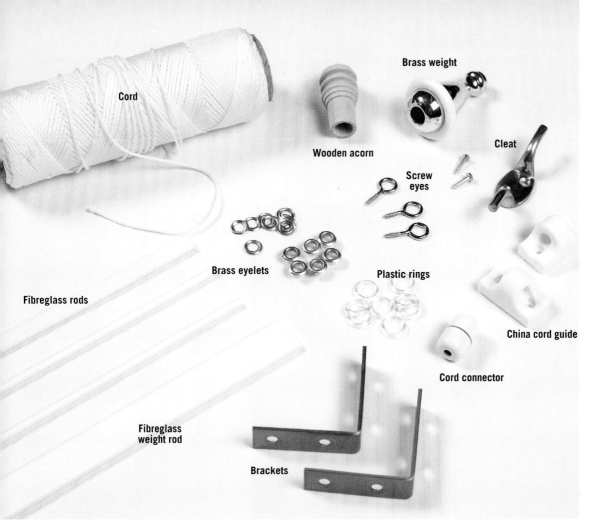

Cord

Brass weight

Wooden acorn

Cleat

Screw eyes

Brass eyelets

Plastic rings

Fibreglass rods

China cord guide

Cord connector

Fibreglass weight rod

Brackets

BLIND SUNDRIES

Blinds will need an array of different sundries and fixings to make them look neat and professional.

- China cord guides are used to guide the pull cords along the top batten. They are gentler on the cords than screw eyes.
- Cord connectors are used for connecting a decorative pull cord to the main guide cords.
- A wall cleat is required for tying off the pull cords when the blind is pulled up.
- Cord weights: brass or wooden acorns are used as a decorative weight on the end of the cords.

- Plastic rings/eyelets are attached to the blind's rod pockets to secure and guide the cords.
- Cords are used to control the rise and fall of the blind.
- 4 mm (⅛ in) rods are inserted into the rod pockets to support the width of the blind's fabric.
- Weight bars: fibreglass bottom weight bars 20 x 4 mm (¾ x ⅛ in) are used to weigh down and support the fall of the blind.
- Brackets are used for fixing the blind's wooden batten in place on or above the window frame.
- Screw eyes are used to guide the pull cords along the blind's wooden batten.

PIPING CORD

Piping cords come in a range of qualities and thicknesses from shoestring to 6 mm (¼ in) diameter.

- Natural cotton has a twist and will shrink when washed.
- Pre-shrunk cotton has a twist.
- Encased: the strands are encased in a fine netting.
- Smooth woven: without a twist.
- Polyprop: a synthetic piping cord without a twist.

SUSPENSION SYSTEMS

There is a wide range of suspension systems used for blinds and curtains. Decorative poles are visibly displayed above the curtain or blind, whereas tracks are usually required to be less obtrusive or hidden behind pelmets or fascias.

TRACKS AND POLES

Tracks and poles come in a range of sizes, shapes and styles to suit almost every need and budget. The most important thing to bear in mind when choosing a track or pole is its suitability for the project in question.

Consideration should be made to:
- Position at the window. Is it to be fitted in the recess of the window, on the frame or above the window?
- Consider its fixings points: top or face fix? Is the fixing point firm enough to secure and hold it firmly?
- Do you want to see the track or does it need to be covered with a pelmet or fascia?
- Consider the weight of the project. Heavy-weight curtains or blinds will need a track system suitable to carry the weight of the fabrics.
- Does it need to be bent to fit the shape of a bay window?
- Will it need to be reverse bent around a corner? Not all tracks and poles can be reverse bent.
- Is the blind to be in constant use? If so, it can be difficult to pull up on a cleat properly and you may prefer to use a chain-operated track system instead.

Remember, it is false economy to buy a cheap system if it is not going to work smoothly and efficiently.

These are just a few examples of suspension systems available:
- Decorative pole.
- Corded track system.
- Un-corded track system.
- Track fitted to a pelmet board.
- Small fascia board.
- Roman blind track systems.
- Roman blind traditional batten.

TIP Poles are there to be seen, but tracks often look unsightly. If you don't want to see the track system, it can be hidden behind a small covered fascia that is just the depth of the track system, or behind a more substantial decorative pelmet. See Pelmets on pages 115–17.

TRACK AND BATTEN SYSTEMS FOR BLINDS

Traditionally, blinds have been fitted to covered wooden battens. This is still a very good and popular system but, today we also have a variety of track systems available, from cord-lock to chain-operated systems. These are very useful for blinds that are to be operated on a regular basis or where children are involved, as they hate wrapping the pull cords around a cleat, often leaving the blinds half drawn and distorted!

When choosing a track system, it is important to check the depth of the track system, including its cord-operating device. These can vary in depth from 4 cm (1½ in) to 10 cm (4 in). You will need to know the depth of the system you choose, in order to accurately calculate the pleat spacings. Also, it is important to know that the system is strong enough to take the weight of the blind, particularly if it is large or made with heavy-weight fabrics.

Whichever system you use, they both have Velcro fitted to the face of the track/batten and, using small brackets, are either face-fixed to the window frame or wall, or can be top-fixed inside the window recess.

COVERED BATTENS

- Traditional wooden battens are made with pieces of wood approximately 5–10 cm (2–4 in) wide by 2.5 cm (1 in) deep.
- The overall length will depend on the size of your blind, but I find that the best results are when the batten is cut 1.5 cm (⅝ in) smaller than the overall width of the blind.
- The batten is covered with lining fabric, and the hook side of Velcro is fixed to the front edge.
- Screw eyes or china cord guides are then fitted to the underside. These should be fitted 7.5 cm (3 in) in from each end, and then evenly spaced about 30 cm (12 in) apart.
- Pull cords are threaded through the cord guides and rings are tied off on the bottom ring/eyelet, using a slip knot. (See Slip knot on page 44.)
- Leave at least 60 cm (2 ft) hanging at the side to which a wooden acorn or brass weight is attached to form the pull. Alternatively, fit a cord connector at the end of the batten with a decorative pull cord attached.

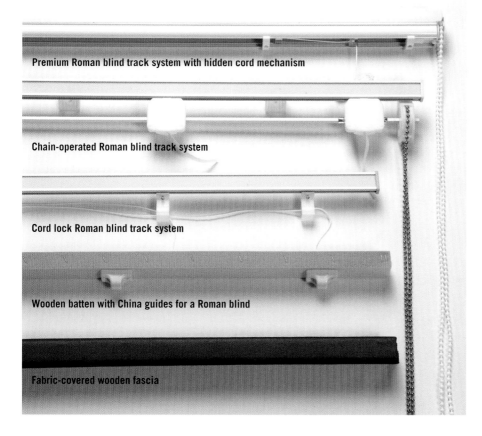

Premium Roman blind track system with hidden cord mechanism

Chain-operated Roman blind track system

Cord lock Roman blind track system

Wooden batten with China guides for a Roman blind

Fabric-covered wooden fascia

FABRICS

There is a glorious array of colours, designs and textured fabrics available today. Having an understanding of their construction and composition will help you determine the best ones to use for your chosen projects. In fact, I think it was my love of fabulous textiles that first fuelled my passion for soft furnishings. I find that inspiration for a scheme comes from the fabrics: once I have found the main fabric, the rest of the scheme comes together quite easily.

Fabrics have been woven for centuries on simple handlooms and the basic formation has not changed much, just the intricacies of design using new and more refined fibres. Fabrics are made by weaving together a series of lateral and vertical threads to form basic plain-woven patterns through to very intricate designs. Therefore, it is important that you understand the make-up and composition of the fabrics. You need to know how they will react in different atmospheric conditions, how the fabric will hang and how to care for them.

FIBRES

Fabric fibres fall into two main categories: natural and man-made.

NATURAL FIBRES AND THEIR PROPERTIES

There are six basic natural fibres that are derived from animal or plant extracts: cotton, linen, silk, wool, viscose and modal. These fibres can be used alone, combined with other natural fibres or combined with a mixture of natural and man-made fibres to produce a huge array of fabrics.

Cotton (from the cotton plant)

- Cotton fibres are fine and soft, and easy to handle.
- Good spinning qualities because of the natural twist in the fibre.
- Abrasion-resistant and durable.
- Absorbs water and 'breathes', but is slow to dry.
- Stronger wet than dry.
- Will shrink unless treated.
- Creases easily.
- Can withstand heat, detergents and bleach.

- Resists static electricity build-up.
- Can be damaged by mildew and prolonged exposure to sunlight.
- Blending with other fibres improves its easy-care and durability.

Linen (stem fibres from the flax plant)

- Linen is the oldest woven fabric in the world.
- Linen fibres have a subdued luster, and do not soil easily or shed lint.
- Long fibres from 15–50 cm (6–20 in) make linen even smoother than cotton.
- Twice the strength of cotton, but less supple.
- Stronger wet than dry.
- Highly absorbent and prone to movement according to atmospheric conditions.
- Creases badly and will shrink. Press whilst still damp.
- Often blended with other fibres and easy-care treatments.
- Linen Union is a fabric with a cotton warp and a linen weft.

Silk (from the silkworm's cocoon)

- Silk culture began in China around 1725 BC and was a carefully-guarded secret for about three thousand years.
- Expensive and most valued for its 'silky' feel.
- Very long filaments (can be as much as a mile long – or 1600 metres!).
- Several cocoons are unwound and carefully twisted together to produce one fine yarn.
- Silkworms fed on mulberry leaves produce a fine fabric.
- Silkworms fed on oak leaves produce a coarser silk called tussah: a rough-textured fabric, usually pale brown or stone coloured.

- Stronger than cotton or linen.
- Can be damaged by chlorine bleach and sunlight.
- Absorbs moisture but dries quickly.
- Is resilient and elastic and resistant to creasing, with wrinkles tending to fall out.
- Requires delicate handling and cleaning.

Wool (from sheep, goats, rabbits, camels, alpacas and lamas)
- Woollen cloth has been made in a variety of types since the Middle Ages.
- Most valued for its textured appearance and warmth.
- Worsted yarns have long and fine staples that produce a smoother, more lustrous cloth.
- Woollen yarns have short staples and produce a softer, bulkier cloth.
- Weaker than cotton or linen, especially when wet.
- Springs back into shape after being crushed or wrinkled.
- Must be washed gently or dry cleaned as it will felt, matt or shrink.
- Can be made machine-washable by chemical treatments.
- Blends well with other fibres to improve durability, reduce felting and aid aftercare.
- Flame-resistant (wool usually extinguishes itself when the source of flame is removed).
- Can be damaged by chlorine bleach.
- Moths and carpet beetles eat wool.
- Does not attract dirt or static electricity.
- The fineness, quality and cost of wool is dependent on the breed of animal that produces it.

Modal and Viscose
- Viscose fibres are produced by extrusion from eucalyptus, pine or beech wood pulp.
- Modal fibres are made by a modified viscose process.
- Both fibres are fine and soft.
- Both crease easily.
- Both are very absorbent and more absorbent than cotton.
- Viscose fibres swell in water, causing it to shrink.
- Modal shrinks less, but both fibres can be treated to reduce shrinkage and improve wrinkle recovery.
- Often blended with other fibres.

SYNTHETIC FIBRES AND THEIR PROPERTIES
Man-made synthetic fibres, derived from petroleum products, are generally thermoplastic, which means they soften or fuse when heated and then harden again when cooled, so they need to be treated with care. These basic fibres can be used alone or combined together to improve the quality, efficiency and cost of the yarn, or to enhance the visual look.

Nylon
- First made in the 1930s.
- Made entirely from mineral sources.
- High tensile strength, is abrasion-resistant and water-repellent.
- Has low resistance to sunlight.

Polyester
- First made in 1941.
- Is strong and resistant to wrinkles, abrasion and light.
- Will collect static, will pill and has a low absorbency.
- Polyester fibres are used alone or mixed with other fibres to produce easy-care fabrics such as polyester cottons.

Acrylic
- First produced in 1952.
- Strong and hard-wearing.
- Handles like wool, but without the problems of shrinking and felting.
- Often blended with other fibres.

Moda-acrylic
- First produced in 1956.
- Similar to acrylic, but withstands higher temperatures and does not burn.
- Especially developed for fire- or flame-retardant fabrics.

WEAVES

Fabric is woven on a loom using a series of warp threads through which the weft thread is passed, from left to right and back again. There are three basic weaves:

Plain or tabby weave, where the warp thread is lifted over alternate weft threads.

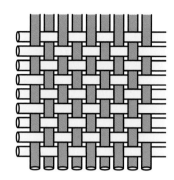

Satin weave, where the warp threads are predominant. The warp floats over four or more wefts and remains under one. Adjacent warps are arranged randomly so as to not appear as twill.

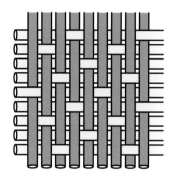

Twill weave, where the warp thread is lifted over more than one weft thread at a time and is displaced by one warp with each additional row giving a diagonal effect.

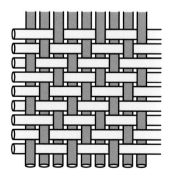

All other effects are achieved by:

- Various combinations of the basic weaves:
  - Hopsack or basket weave is produced when two or more warps are raised or lowered alternately to create a chequered appearance.
  - Herringbone weave is made by reversing the direction of the twill at regular intervals, often enhanced by using different coloured warp and weft threads.
  - Sateen weave is as a satin but the weft thread is predominant.
- Using special groupings of yarn in either the warp or weft.
- Using yarns of unequal size, or 'fancy' yarns.
- Adding extra warps or wefts to allow pile or loops, or 'double cloth' (see Glossary on page 156).
- With the aid of special loom attachments:

Dobby

- Dobby weave consists of small, simple geometric repeat patterns produced on a dobby loom invented in 1824.

– Jacquard is an intricate design that can be produced on a Jacquard loom, invented in 1802 by Joseph Marie Jacquard. The jacquard attachment to a loom uses a series of punched cards to select the warp threads and to raise them when necessary, producing multi-coloured complex designs.

Jacquard

Sheers, voiles and lace

From these weaves, fabrics can then be grouped together:

Cottons
- Calico
- Canvas
- Chintz
- Crewel
- Denim
- Toile de Jouy

Silks
- Dupions
- Sateen
- Satin
- Shot silk
- Taffeta
- Tussah

Wools
- Knitted: weft knitting can be done by hand or machine but warp knitting is purely a machine process
- Tapestry
- Tartan
- Tweed

Pile fabrics
- Chenille
- Corduroy
- Moquette
- Plush
- Velour
- Velvet
- Velveteen

Decorative
- Brocade
- Brocatelle
- Damask
- Embroidered
- Gaufragé (embossed)
- Matelassé
- Moiré
- Repp

Sheers, voiles and lace
Made from a range of natural and/or man-made fibres to produce fine plain and decorative fabrics.

FABRIC DIRECTORY

The choice of fabric is huge and, therefore, careful consideration should be given to the fabrics you choose for your various projects. Not all fabrics are suitable for all applications. Consider the fabric's weave and structure, its weight and handling, its durability, any special treatments required and its visual appeal: colour, pattern and texture, as well as its end use.

Brocatelle is a heavy-figured cloth with a relief pattern, often with large foliate patterns in a satin weave surrounded by a tightly-woven background. Woven on a Jacquard loom, the cloth has extra weft threads to pad out the pattern, producing a high relief. Satin weave forms the pattern on the warp, with a plain weft background. Originally made in silk and linen but now made using a variety of fibres.

Brocade is a finely-woven decorative fabric that uses a variety of weaves on a Jacquard loom. Patterns are formed by one or more weft threads floating on the back of the fabric and being brought through to the surface when required. The wrong side of the fabric is easy to distinguish by the floating weft threads. Brocades are rich, colourful fabrics that were traditionally made from silk, often hand embroidered, and perfected during the 16th and 17th centuries in France, Italy and Spain. Today, many fibre blends are used to create a wide variety of fabrics.

Chenille, often referred to as 'poor man's velvet', comes from the French word for caterpillar, which is what it resembles. The fibre is produced with a fuzzy pile-like fringe, which is woven into the weave of the fabric. Chenille fabrics are often used for furnishings and upholstery but can 'seat' under pressure to give different shadings.

Chintz is a fine, plain-woven cotton fabric, originally a painted or stained calico from India. Modern chintz is usually made up of bright prints on a light background. Today, the word chintz is used to describe any patterned or plain-glazed or semi-glazed fabric used in soft furnishings.

Crewel fabrics are plain- or hopsack-woven natural linen or cotton background fabrics, which are embroidered with wool in chain stitch and French knots. Crewelwork fabrics were very fashionable during the 17th and 18th centuries, depicting birds, animals and flowers, and were mainly used for bed hangings. Many modern crewelwork fabrics are now made in India, and are used for bedding and curtains.

Corduroy is a cut ribbed pile fabric with lengthways ridges or cords that may vary from fine to wide. Extra filling weft yarns float over a number of warp yarns. After the fabric is woven, the floating yarns are cut, and the pile is brushed and singed to produce a clear cord effect. Corded fabrics were fashionable during Victorian times, often with much heavier cords than used today. Originally a cotton fabric, it is now made with a range of fibres.

Damask is a monochrome reversible, soft, glossy fabric woven on a Jacquard loom to form a self-pattern: formed by the satin-weave background and the matt sateen-weave figuring. Traditional motifs include flowers, foliage and exotic fruits, sometimes with the addition of gold or silver threads.

Damask was first produced in the Syrian capital, Damascus, during the 4th century. The first European damasks were made in Italy during the 15th century, but by the 17th century production had spread to France. Following the French Huguenots migration to England, large quantities were produced and sustained throughout the 18th century. Originally made of silk but today we use a range of fibres to make damask fabrics.

Denim originally woven in Nîmes, South of France, is a 2:1 or 3:1 twill weave formation woven using a hard-wearing twist cotton yarn dyed indigo blue.

Matelassé is from the French *matelasser* which means to quilt or wad. Produced on a Jacquard loom, a matelassé is a double-woven damask fabric with a figured relief effect, which looks like machine quilting. The designs are formed by a mix of floating threads, weaves and stitches that stitch the front and back cloths together at intervals.

Doupion is a plain-woven fabric made from rough, irregular silk yarns. Doupion means a double cocoon, where silk was spun from two cocoons that were nested together and not separated in spinning. Silk reeled from such cocoons is very irregular. Doupions are normally made from silk, but viscose, acetate and other synthetic yarns are also used today.

Moquette (mock velvet) is a warp-looped pile fabric, which may have a cut or uncut pile, or a combination of both, with several colours forming designs. Very popular during the 1940s and '50s, it is a very durable upholstery fabric often used on public transport seating.

Moiré is a very fine-ribbed fabric fashionable since the early 18th century. Moiré is usually silk, cotton or man-made fibres such as rayon, that have been finished by calendaring (passing between heavy iron or copper rollers) to produce a watery appearance simulating water reflections.

Repp is a plain-weave fabric with a very dominant rib running in the weft direction, with finer, more numerous, warp yarns. Repp is a traditional fabric produced in good-quality cotton or wool for curtains, loose covers and the heavier weights for upholstery.

Plush is taken from the French *peluche*, meaning shaggy or hairy. It is a heavy fabric with a long pile of more than 3 mm (⅛ in), produced for upholstery and some clothing. The pile is less dense than in velvet, but can be long enough to simulate fur. Plush was very popular during the first half of the 20th century as a durable wool or mohair pile cover with cotton or rayon as a base. It is used in domestic and contract seating, particularly theatre and cinema seating.

Sateen is the reverse construction to satin weave. A five- or eight-warp satin weave where the weft thread is on the face of the fabric.

Satin is a very smooth fabric on the right side, produced by weaving in an interlaced pattern. The warp threads are generally much finer than the weft threads, and are numerous to the square inch so that they conceal the weft and make an unbroken, smooth and lustrous surface. Satin-weave fabrics are made from all types of yarn.

Taffeta is a smooth, plain-weave fabric made from even lightweight yarns with a shiny filament, which give the fabric a sheen to produce a firm, crisp fabric. Originally made of silk, but now also made with man-made fibres.

Shot silk is a plain weave using lustrous yarns. The shot effect is created by using different coloured yarns in the warp and weft, producing an iridescent effect.

Tapestry. The word tapestry is derived from the French word *tapis*, meaning carpet or covering. A durable material similar in appearance to embroidery. Early tapestries were handmade needlework fabrics produced from cotton, linen and wool, with the weft threads being threaded into the warps with fingers or a bobbin. There are different styles of tapestry cloths, from traditional pictorial scenes used during the Middle Ages for wall hangings, to more contemporary geometric designs. Tapestry is a heavy fabric used for upholstery and curtains. Imitation machine-made tapestries are heavy, closely-woven patterned fabrics woven on a Jacquard loom.

Tartan. Traditionally, tartan cloths are made of wool in a twill weave woven with different-coloured stripes crossing at right angles. Each tartan design belongs to an individual Scottish clan.

Tweed is generally a heavyweight all-wool cloth produced in various weaves, plain or twill, and may have a check or herringbone pattern with a smooth or rough surface. Often, the warp and weft have contrasting colours, and different effects are obtained by twisting together different coloured woollen fibres into two- or three-ply yarn. Harris Tweed is well known for its durability.

Toile de Jouy was created in France in 1760 and manufactured from 1770 to 1843 at Jouy, near Paris. A plain-woven cotton fabric with both flower motifs and the characteristic pastoral and romanticized rustic courtship scenes printed in single colours.

Velvet is a soft, thick, short-pile fabric of no more than 3 mm (⅛ in). Originally of silk with a plain twill or satin weave cotton ground. The quality is determined by the closeness of the tufts and density and construction of the backing. The pile surface is formed by weaving an extra set of warp threads that are looped over wires, the rods being withdrawn after the weft thread is placed, leaving a row of loops or tufts across the breadth. The loops may remain uncut, forming terry velvet, or cut automatically in machine weaving or by a special tool in hand looming. The fabric may also be woven double, face-to-face, and then cut apart.

Magnificent velvets were produced in Europe in the 12th and 13th centuries for religious and court ceremonials. Lucca and Genoa in Italy were the first cities to make fine velvets and excelled through the 16th and 17th centuries. Silk Genoa velvets made since the Renaissance have always been the most expensive. Utrecht or mohair velvets are made from the wool of the Angora goat. They are less costly, rich, stout velvets made of linen warp and weft with a pile of the Angora goat's hair, used for wall and furniture coverings. Victorian velvets were normally on a black ground cloth. Modern velvets are of many types and grades.

Gaufragé velvets have patterns embossed on them by a heated roller process.

Velveteen is an all-over short, closely set, weft pile that slopes slightly, creating a slight sheen.

Velour is taken from the French word for velvet and is a short warp pile cloth with a good, dense pile, closely woven from cotton. Velour pile is laid in one direction, usually down the length of the roll, giving the surface a distinct shading. Produced in several weights for curtaining and upholstery.

FABRIC CARE

Today's fabrics are made using a variety of fibres. Careful attention to their care is needed in order to maintain their look and feel.

Curtains and drapes do not need to be washed on a regular basis. These fabrics should be handled as little as possible. It is the moisture in your hands that attracts dirt to these fabrics. The use of draw rods, rather than your hands, to pull curtains will help alleviate this problem and will extend the time between cleaning. Too much washing or cleaning will wash out the dressings and treatments in fabrics, making them look limp and lifeless. A light vacuum on a regular basis to remove dust is all that is generally needed.

CARE INSTRUCTIONS

Care symbols give an indication of the recommended care procedures, which, if followed, should avoid the risk of damage.

NOTE: A cross through a symbol means 'DO NOT'.

  Hot wash:
White cotton or linen without special finishes.

  60°C:
Cotton, linen, modal, polyester and their blends where colours and finishes are fast at 60°C.

 40°C:
Cotton or polyester in deep colours.

  40°C, gentle program:
Delicate fabrics of modal, viscose, acrylics, polyester, nylon.

 30° C, gentle program:
Shrink-resistant wool, acetate.

 Hand wash:
Normal wool, silk.

 Do not wash:
Very delicate wool and silk fabrics.

 May be chlorine bleached.

 Do not use chlorine bleach.

 Cotton, linen.

 Wool, silk, polyester, viscose.

 Acrylic, nylon, acetate.

 Polypropylene.

 No limitations on the use of dry-cleaning solvents.

    Limitations.

 Do not dry clean.

  The divisions are similar to those for washing and ironing. Fabrics made from wool, silk and acrylics, and knitted fabrics susceptible to shrinking or stretching are not suitable for tumble drying.

FABRIC CHARACTERISTICS

Most curtain fabrics are 137 cm (54 in) wide but some, such as silk, often come up a lot smaller at 112 cm (44 in) so you need to be aware of this as it could affect the quantity of fabric required.

All fabrics have a selvedge on each side. On some woven fabrics this can be very small, but on printed fabrics it can be quite large with printing information running down the side.

The selvedge can sometimes be quite tight, and it may be necessary to snip it in order to release any tension.

When you order fabric always check, before you cut it, that you have the right fabric, colour and quantity, and that it is free from faults. Once cut, the manufacturer will not take responsibility for it.

When cutting out fabric, first mark the position of the cuts with pins, so as to be sure that you have the right quantity of fabric and that you have taken the appropriate steps to account for any pattern repeat. Use a setsquare and long ruler when marking up and cutting out fabrics.

Always try to mark fabrics on the wrong side, as it can be very difficult to get chalk marks out. If you make a mistake, it won't be a problem if the marks are on the wrong side.

Check that any lining fabrics are the same width as the curtain fabric, as they may vary and you may need to cut extra lengths of lining fabric to account for the width of the curtain fabric.

With plain and some symmetrical patterns it may be possible to dovetail smaller pieces together, but this will not be possible with fabrics that have a one-way pattern or a pile with a nap to it.

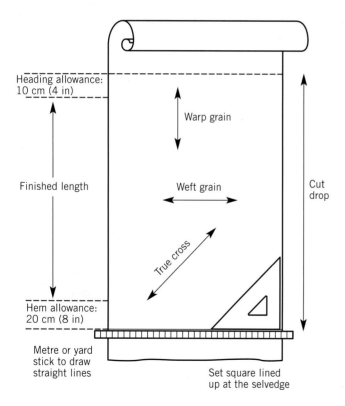

Heading allowance: 10 cm (4 in)

Warp grain

Finished length

Weft grain

Cut drop

True cross

Hem allowance: 20 cm (8 in)

Metre or yard stick to draw straight lines

Set square lined up at the selvedge

TIP With some fabrics it can be difficult to tell the difference between the right side and the wrong side of the fabric. Often the manufacturer will identify the front of the fabric, but if you are unsure ask your customer to identify and mark the side they want you to use. This will avoid the risk of expensive misunderstandings if the incorrect side is used.

PATTERNED FABRIC

The design on fabric is usually printed across the width of the fabric and is then repeated at intervals along its length. This is called the 'pattern repeat'. However, some fabrics, such as sheers and voiles, are produced as 'room highs' i.e. 285 cm to 3 m (9 ft 4 in to 9 ft 8 in) high, and then you measure off the amount required across the width. This avoids seams being visible across the width of sheer fabrics.

Similarly, some fabrics are produced as 'rail road', often striped or upholstery weights, where the fabric is produced with the selvedge at the top and bottom of the pattern/stripe. This is particularly useful when upholstering or making loose covers for sofas as it avoids the need for seams being visible on the backs.

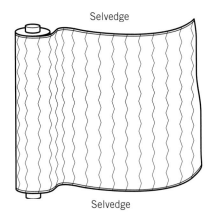

Selvedge

Selvedge

PATTERN MATCHING

Most fabrics, but not all, can be easily pattern-matched from one side to the other. Printed fabrics will, more often than not, give you a 6 mm (¼ in) overlap of pattern, which will allow you to pattern-match when working from the wrong side of the fabric, but this may not be the case with some woven fabrics. See Joining patterned fabrics on page 37.

TIP Always check the designs on fabrics very carefully as their characteristics may not always be obvious at first glance and they can throw up some additional problems such as pattern and pleating alignment.

Never try to pattern-match striped fabric down the line between two stripes. It is almost impossible to sew a completely accurate line. Therefore, you are far better to join your fabrics down the body of a stripe, as the join will be less obtrusive.

PATTERN FORMATIONS

There are four basic pattern formations:

Full-drop pattern repeat laid out symmetrically (i.e. mirror imaged from the centre).

Pattern repeat

Full-drop pattern repeat laid out symmetrically on the fabric but with an asymmetric design (i.e. designs all learning one-way).

Half-drop pattern repeat with a symmetric design.

Pattern repeat

Half-drop pattern repeat with an asymmetric design.

In this final instance, care will need to be taken when considering the chosen window design. Bold patterns or colours on an asymmetric design will mean that the leading edges on a pair of curtains will not match up if you follow the true pattern repeat. Therefore, you should consider what looks best.

True pattern repeat

If your fabric has a bright flower leaning to the right, it will show a bold design leaning to the leading edge of the left-hand curtain, but it will lean away from the leading edge of the right-hand curtain, giving the effect of a bright edge on one curtain and not on the other.

If this is the case, you need to decide which effect you prefer. Ask yourself what would look best during the day when the curtains are drawn back, and then compare with the effect at night when the curtains are closed together. I recommend that you go with what looks best during the day, as curtains are drawn back for longer periods than are closed together.

Leading edge pattern alignment

By adding an extra half-drop pattern repeat to one curtain, the pattern lines up with two evenly bold leading edges when drawn back, but when closed together the design still lines up but, technically, the pattern is misaligned.

PATTERN LAYOUT

Generally, it is better to cut fabric with a full pattern at the bottom of the curtain. Half patterns are less obvious and can be lost in the heading.

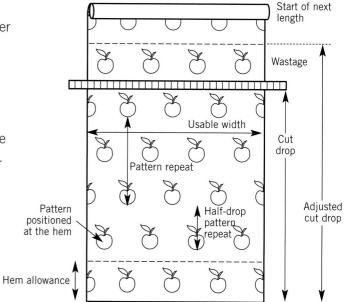

When seaming widths of fabric together for curtains, any half widths should always be added to the back edge of the curtains.

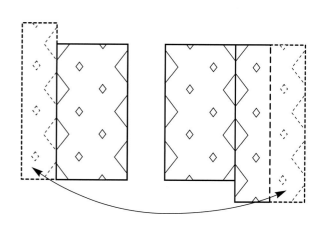

When odd widths are required in a pair of curtains, always cut the final drop one whole pattern repeat longer, so that when it is cut down the centre and each half joined to its appropriate side, the excess can be cut away from the top of one and the bottom of the other.

Similarly, if you need to join fabrics together for blinds or pelmets, you should try to have a full width in the centre and any additional fabric required should be added equally on either side. However, this is not always possible with a large asymmetric pattern. In this case, you need to make a judgement as to what looks best: the dominant pattern being centred with the seams unequal or equal seams?

JOINING PATTERNED FABRIC

Generally, if you are using a printed fabric, it will have a 6 mm (¼ in) overlap of the pattern for pattern matching.

Pattern matching

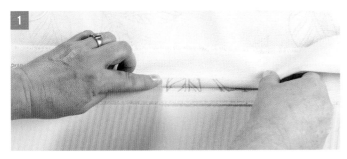

1 Turn one side of the fabric over and iron in a crease 6 mm (¼ in) from the edge of the pattern. Line up with the 6 mm (¼ in) overlap of pattern on the other side of the fabric.

2 Turn the fold back and pin into the crease mark. Machine stitch in place.

TIP On difficult or slippery fabrics it is better to slip tack the fabrics together before machining. See slip tacking (right).

Slip tacking

Slip tacking is used when pattern-matching difficult or slippery fabrics.

1 Fold in and crease 6 mm (¼ in) from the edge of the pattern on one side of the fabric. Match the pattern of the folded edge with the pattern on the other piece of fabric and pin in place. Pass the needle, in line with the folded edge, through the fabric for approximately 2.5 cm (1 in). Where the needle comes out, cross to the folded edge of the fabric and pass the needle through the folded edge of the fabric for approximately 2.5 cm (1 in). Continue up the length of the fabrics.

2 On the wrong side of the fabric, turn the folded edge back to reveal the stitching underneath and machine stitch down the crease of the fold.

MEASURING AND ESTIMATING FABRICS

With all your soft furnishings projects it is very important to take accurate measurements and to estimate the correct amount of materials required. Incorrect measurements and fabric quantities can be a very expensive mistake.

1) When taking measurements always make sure they are accurate. Allowances can be added later. Complete a measuring chart (see page 39) for future reference.
2) Take your time when taking measurements. Take all the measurements possible, regardless of the window treatment you are planning. If you have taken all possible measurements in the first instance, you can cross-check your figures and you will save yourself a return journey to re-measure.

> **TIP** The most important aspect of measuring and estimating fabrics is accuracy. Accuracy of measurements and accuracy in the cutting of fabrics. **Measure twice, cut once!**

3) Take someone with you when measuring large or awkward windows, as it may not be possible for your client to climb a stepladder to reach the required heights.
4) Be careful of your customer's ornaments and furniture. Ask that they be moved or removed to give you clear access when taking measurements. This may be tiresome but is preferable to damaging something or injuring yourself by overreaching.
5) When measuring for blinds or curtains to be fitted inside the window recess, always take three measurements each way: top, middle and bottom as well as left, right and centre, as windows are rarely square. Also, you will often find that the plaster on the inside of a window recess is thicker on the front edge than the back. So, if a track or blind is to be fitted flush with the front edge of the window recess, make sure you measure that edge or it may not fit.
6) Remember to take account of window furniture such as window catches and locks, etc.
7) Once you have taken your measurements transfer the relevant information to a cutting plan so that you can make an estimate of the fabric requirements.

MEASURING WINDOWS

When taking measurements, always take them in three places: top, middle and bottom, as well as left, right and centre, and use the smaller of these measurements, particularly when fitting into the window recess.

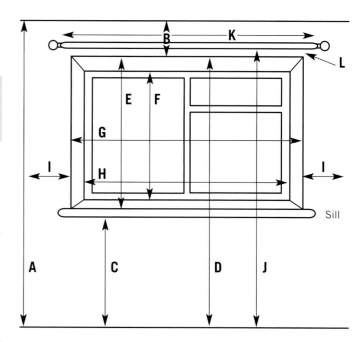

A = Floor to ceiling/coving
B = Top of window to ceiling/coving
C = Sill to floor
D = Top of window to floor
E = Height of window, including architrave
F = Height of window recess
G = Width of window, including architrave
H = Width of window recess
I = Space on either side of the window to allow for curtain stack-back
J = Track/pole suspension point to floor/sill length
K = Width of track/pole
L = Depth of track/pole (top to suspension point)

> **TIP** Take a camera with you to make a visual record, particularly of any difficult angles or problem areas.

MEASURING CHART

CUSTOMER DETAILS:

ROOM/DESIGN SPECIFICATION:

FABRIC DETAILS inc. pattern repeat

	Window 1	Window 2	Window 3	Window 4	Window 5
A = Floor to ceiling/coving					
B = Top of window to ceiling/coving					
C = Sill to floor					
D = Top of window to floor					
E = Height of window, including architrave					
F = Height of window recess					
G = Width of window, including architrave					
H = Width of window recess					
I = Space either side of window: Left side Right side					
J = Track/pole suspension point to floor/sill length					
K = Width of track/pole					
L = Depth of track/pole (top to suspension point)					
Pelmet board: Width Depth Return					
Other information: * Track overlap * Height of track/pole above the window * Depth of window sill/recess					

NOTES: (Flooring/radiators/window catches/obstacles, etc.)

CUTTING PLAN

When estimating the fabric requirements, always produce a cutting plan based on plain fabric. If a patterned fabric is then chosen, you will need to reproduce the cutting plan taking into account any pattern repeat over 10 cm (4 in). A pattern repeat of less than 10 cm (4 in) can usually be accommodated within the allowances.

Box cushion example:
Fabric width = 137 cm (54 in)

CUSHION TOP 60 cm (2 ft)	CUSHION BOTTOM 60 cm (2 ft)
CUSHION BORDER 13 cm (5 in)	
CUSHION BORDER 13 cm (5 in)	
ZIP BORDER	8 cm (3¼ in)
PIPING 50 cm (20 in)	

Total fabric requirements for plain fabric = 1.5 m (5 ft)

SEWING TECHNIQUES

There are a few basic sewing techniques: stitches, seams, knots, chain bars, mitres, weight covers and cord pockets that are used again and again throughout most soft furnishing projects. Once you have mastered these basics they can be adapted according to the different applications.

STITCHES

Unless otherwise stated, seam allowances are always 1.5 cm (⅝ in). Do not forget that in most instances you will need a seam allowance on each side of your work.

> **TIP** Your work will be made easier and will look its best if you remember to be accurate in your measuring and cutting, and in the neatness of your stitching.

Lock stitch

Lock stitch is used to tie the lining, interlining and fabric together, but still allowing for slight movement.

1 Using a long length of thread that matches the colour of the fabric and starting from the hem, take a tiny stitch through the lining or interlining and then through the fabric. These stitches must be barely visible on the front of the fabric.

2 Make a loop in the thread about 20 cm (8 in) up and take another small stitch through the lining or interlining and the fabric.

3 Continue up the length of the curtain, stopping approximately 25 cm (10 in) from the top of the curtain, so as to not interfere with the heading that will be worked later.

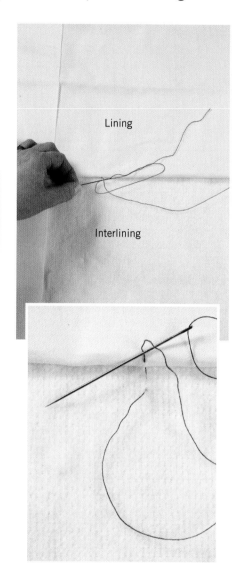

Lining

Interlining

Serge stitch

Serge stitch is a long stitch, barely visible on the front of the fabric, used to hold the folded edge of the fabric in place. These stitches should be placed close to the raw edge, no more than 5 cm (2 in) long, and should not be visible when covered by the lining fabric. If interlining is being used, these stitches only go through the interlining and not through to the front of the fabric.

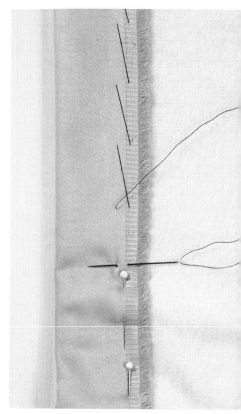

Herringbone stitch

Herringbone stitch is used for hemming: stitching the fabric of the hem to the interlining, using stitches approximately 1.5 cm (⅝ in) long. These stitches should not go through to the front of the fabric.

If you are right-handed, the stitch is worked from left to right, with the needle pointing to the left as you work the stitch. If you are left-handed, work from right to left.

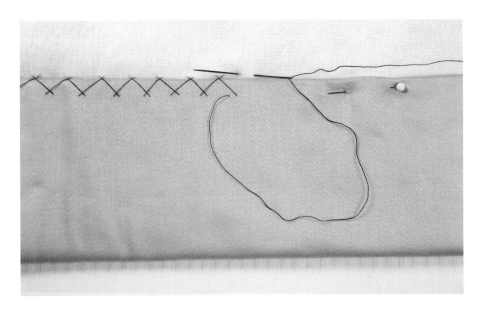

Blind hem stitch

A hand-stitched blind hem is used on unlined curtains and sheers. It allows the fold of the hem to lie back away from the fabric, giving a cleaner line on the front of the fabric. A tiny stitch will be visible on the front of the fabric.

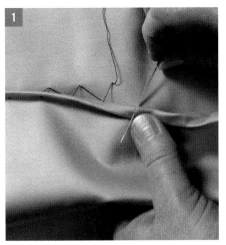

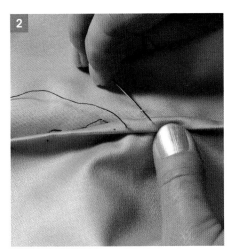

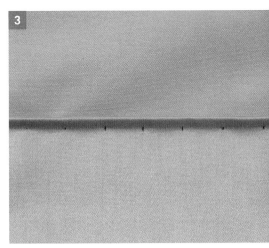

1 This stitch is worked in a similar way to herringbone stitch, but the threads do not cross. If you are right-handed, work from left to right; if you are left-handed, work from right to left. Roll back the top edge of the hem 6 mm (¼ in) and take a stitch at right angles to the hem. Make sure you go through all the layers of the hem fabric.

2 Move along approximately 1 cm (⅜ in) and take a tiny stitch through the main fabric.

3 Move along a further 1 cm (⅜ in) and take a stitch through the hem, as in Step 1. Continue the length of the hem.

Slip stitch (ladder stitch)

Slip stitch is a small stitch between 6 mm (¼ in) to 1.5 cm (⅝ in) long that is used where two fabrics meet, when at least one has a folded edge. Slip stitch in upholstery and soft furnishings is slightly different to slip stitch used in dressmaking. Dressmakers often refer to this stitch as ladder or turret stitch, but for the purposes of this book, all reference to slip stitch will be worked in this way:

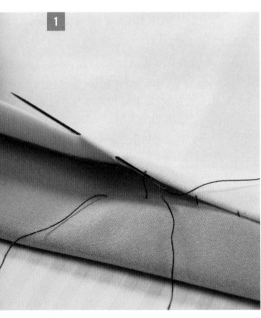

1 **Pass the needle through the fold of the fabric for approximately 1.5 cm (⅝ in). Where it comes out, cross to the opposite fabric and pass the needle through the fabric for approximately 1.5 cm (⅝ in) parallel with the folded edge. Repeat for the full length required. When done properly, you should not see any stitches. However, if you don't go directly into the opposite fabric each time, you will see a small slanting stitch.**

Stab stitch

Stab stitch is formed by making three or four small stitches one on top of the other and is used to hold layers of fabric together as unobtrusively as possible.

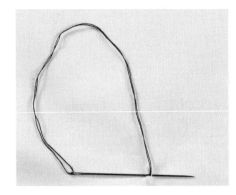

Buttonhole stitch

Buttonhole stitch is a neat top stitch used when sewing rings onto the back of blinds and tie-backs.

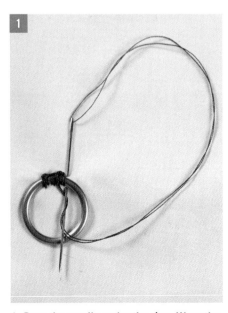

1 **Pass the needle under the ring. Wrap the thread around the needle twice and pull tight. Place the next stitch close to the last. Continue as required.**

Securing stitch

I find this the best way of finishing off and securing the thread:

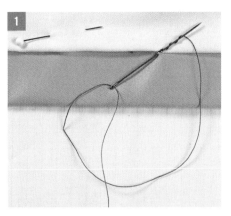

1 **Take a couple of small stitches on the spot. Then take a small stitch and pass the thread around the needle a couple of times. Pull tight to secure.**

MACHINE STITCHES

You only really need to use two basic machine stitches: straight and zigzag. However, if your machine has some decorative stitches, these can be used to enhance any decorative detailing.

Straight stitch

Most domestic sewing machines are set up for dressmaking and, therefore, the stitch length is generally a bit small for soft furnishings. I recommend that you increase your stitch length to 3.5 or 4 to give a good, even stitch length without puckering.

Always start machine stitching with the needle down in the fabric; this will help avoid 'snatch-back'. Alternatively, you can hold the threads tight as you start to machine stitch.

Never push or pull the work through the machine, just hold and guide the fabric through the machine.

If you find your seam looks puckered it could be because of a number of things:

- The needle is blunt or damaged – check and renew your needle regularly.
- Use the correct needle and thread for the weight of the fabric.
- The tension is too tight.

> **TIP** If you need to machine stitch in the same place more than once (when attaching piping for instance), increase the stitch length slightly with each additional row of stitching.

Zigzag stitch
Zigzag stitch is used to neaten seams and raw edges and for gathering. It can also be used as a decorative stitch.

Satin stitch
When the zigzag stitch length is reduced it forms a satin stitch. This is an ideal stitch for machine appliqué.

Securing machine stitches
When starting and ending a row of machines stitches, it is best to do a few forward and reverse stitches to secure the ends.

> **TIP** If you need a particular seam allowance and your machine does not have a marked guide plate, use a piece of masking tape positioned at the required distance from the needle, as your guide.

SEAMS

There are four basic seams that will see you through most soft furnishing projects.

Pinning
When putting two pieces of fabric together, hold them with pins. Place the pins at right angles to the raw edge. This will hold the fabrics together without the fabric slipping up and down the pins, which can move the fabric out of alignment – a problem when pattern matching fabrics.

Flat seam
This is the basic seam used when joining two pieces of fabric together. However, if you are using interlining or wadding, it is best to use a single lapped seam (see right).

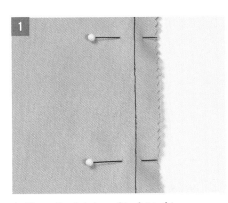

1 **Place the fabrics with right sides together and pin into position. Machine stitch in place using a straight stitch and a seam allowance of 1.5 cm (⅝ in) from the raw edge. Once machined in place, open the seam allowance and press flat.**

> **TIP** If your fabric shows seam marks on the right side of the fabric, re-press under the seam allowance.

Single lapped seam
When joining two pieces of interlining or wadding together, it is better to use a single lapped seam to avoid unnecessary bulk.

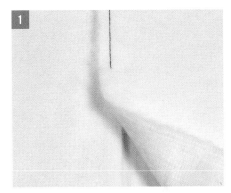

1 **Overlap the edges of the interlining by 1.5 cm (⅝ in) and machine or hand stitch down the centre of the overlap.**

French seam
A French seam is ideal for joining sheer fabrics or unlined curtain fabric when you don't want to see any raw edges.

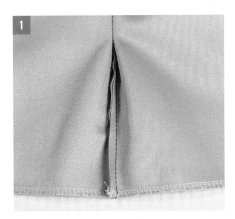

1 **Pin the fabrics with wrong sides together and machine stitch 6 mm (¼ in) from the raw edge. Trim away any fibres and turn the fabric through so that right sides are together. Machine stitch in place 1 cm (⅜ in) in, enclosing all the raw edges. Press all seams one way from the right side of the fabric.**

Flat fell seam

The flat fell seam is used to seam heavier weight fabrics, enclosing all raw edges.

1 Pin the fabrics together with right sides together. Machine stitch a 3 cm (1¼ in) seam allowance. Trim one side of the seam allowance only to half its width. Turn the other side of the seam allowance over, fold the raw edge under and pin in place. Machine stitch close to the folded edge.

Self-bound edge

A self-bound edge is used to enclose the raw edges when frills are attached to unlined and sheer fabrics.

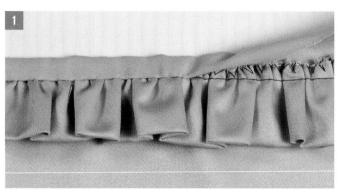

1 Pin the frill to the main fabric 3 cm (1¼ in) from the raw edge. Machine stitch in place 1.5 cm (⅝ in) from the raw edge of the frill. Trim the raw edge of the frill to 1 cm (⅜ in). Fold over the 3 cm (1¼ in) seam allowance of the main fabric and turn under the raw edge. Slip stitch, by hand, using small stitches, or machine stitch in place close to the folded edge, but still within the seam allowance. Make sure the machine stitches do not go through to the right side of the fabric.

SLIP KNOT

A slip knot is used to tie off the guide cords on the back of blinds.

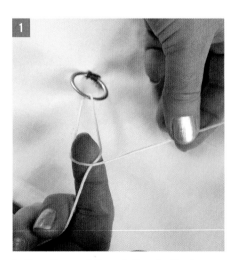

1 Pass the cord through the plastic ring or eyelet. Hold the two threads between thumb and forefinger forming a St Andrew's cross.

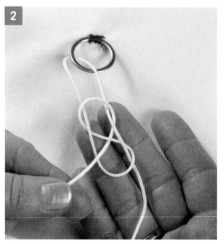

2 Pass the short end around the back of the threads, round the front and to the back again. Take your finger out of the loop and pass the short end through the loop.

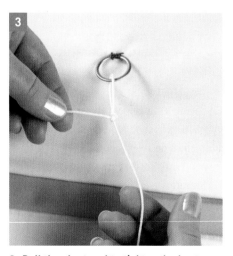

3 Pull the short end to tighten the knot. Pull the long end to slip the knot down the cord.

CHAIN BARS

The chain bar is a length of chain stitches about 7.5 cm (3 in) long that attaches the hem of the lining fabric to the hem of the curtain. The chain bar allows movement in the fabrics but stops the fabrics from billowing out when the window is open. Chain bars are formed at every seam and every half-width of fabric:

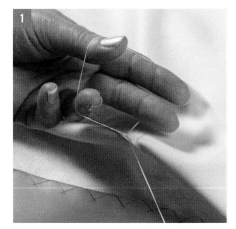

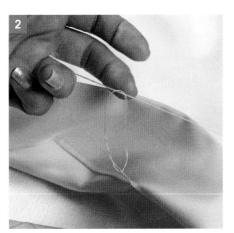

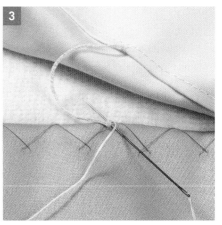

1 Using a long double length of thread, take a stitch in the top of the lining's hem. Then take another stitch in the same place, but instead of pulling the stitch right through, hold the thread tight and form a loop around your thumb and first three fingers on your left hand.

2 Pull the thread through the loop and release the first loop to form a second loop. Pull the thread through the loop and release the second loop to form the next loop. Continue until the chain bar is about 7.5 cm (3 in) long. Pass the needle through the loop to secure the chain bar.

3 Now take a couple of stitches in the top of the hem of the main fabric and secure the chain bar in place between the hems of the lining and the main fabric.

CORNER WEIGHT COVERS

I always cover corner weights as the fabric cover protects expensive fabrics and makes it easier to stitch the weights into the corners of your curtains. I make up batches of corner weights using off-cuts of lining fabric. I then cut them off, as required.

1 To make corner weights, fold a piece of lining fabric in half and machine stitch down one side.

2 Measure 4 cm (1½ in) over and place another row of stitches.

3 6 mm (¼ in) from this row place another row of machine stitches. Continue to place these two rows of stitches across the width of the fabric.

4 Place a corner weight into each channel and machine stitch across the top of this row of corner weights and again 6 mm (¼ in) above this.

5 Place a further row of corner weights in the channels and machine across the top with a second row of stitches just above that. Continue until you have filled all the channels. Now you can cut off the covered corner weights as and when you need them.

CORD POCKETS

Cord pockets are a neat way of enclosing the cords when using commercial heading tapes.

1 Cut a piece of lining fabric 20 cm (8 in) deep by 15 cm (6 in) wide. Fold in half lengthways, and machine stitch across one end and down the side 6 mm (¼ in) from the raw edges. Turn the fabric through to the right side and iron neatly.

2 Turn the closed end up 9 cm (3½ in) and machine stitch up and down the two sides as shown.

3 Place the top raw edges under the heading tape in line with the edge of the lining fabric, and machine in place when machining the heading tape in place.

MITRES

Mitres are used to give neat square corners without any raw edges showing. There are four basic mitres.

True mitre
When the true mitre is used, you will have a small seam at a 45° angle to the corner. The true mitre is ideal for use when both sides of the fabric are equal, but if the side is narrower than the hem there will be a small triangle between the side and hem turnings.

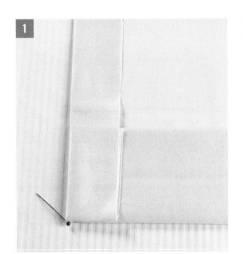

1 Turn the hem up with a double 10 cm (4 in) fold. Turn the side in 5 cm (2 in). Place a pin in the corner. Turn the hem back one fold only and turn the side fold out.

2 Fold the corner in diagonally at the pin so that the side edge is parallel to the hem (this will give you a small allowance ideal for stitching corner weights too).

3 Fold the hem back up and the side back in, so that they meet neatly at a 45° angle to the corner. Slip stitch closed.

Long mitre

The long mitre is used when both edges are of unequal widths, and when you don't want the small triangle between hem and side to be visible. This is best used on unlined curtains and when light coloured fabrics are used on sill-length curtains, when the sun may show the triangular cutout through the fabric.

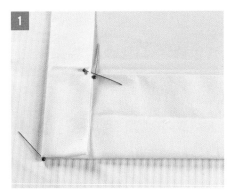

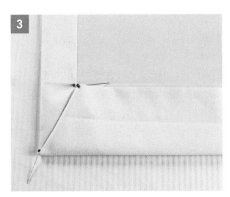

1 Turn the hem up with a double 10 cm (4 in) fold. Turn the side in 5 cm (2 in). Place a pin in the corner, another in the top of the hem where it meets the side fabric, and a third in the side fabric where it meets the hem. Turn the hem back one fold and the side fabric out.

2 Turn the corner fabric in to form a fold, lining up the three pins.

3 Turn the hem and the side seam back in, to form a mitre at a 60° angle to the hem. Slip stitch closed.

Quick mitre

The quick mitre is used when the raw edges are going to be hidden under something else, such as at the corners under heading tape.

1 Fold the edge over and turn the corner fabric in at a 45° angle. If necessary, cut out any excess fabric to reduce bulk. Cover with the heading tape and machine stitch in place.

Double mitre

The double mitre is used on borders around curtains, blinds, tablecloths, bedspreads and tablemats.

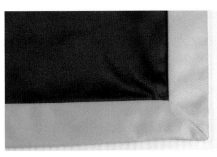

1 Cut out, on the straight of grain, the length of border required for each side by double the depth plus 1.5 cm (⅝ in) seam allowance on each side. Press in a 1.5 cm (⅝ in) seam allowance along the long edges, onto the wrong side of the fabric.

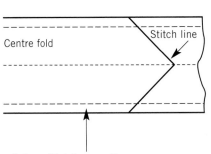

Centre fold

Stitch line

1.5 cm (⅝ in) seam allowance

2 Fold each border piece in half and press in a centre fold line. Mark a 45° stitching line either side of the centre fold line. Machine stitch the two pieces together along the marked stitch line. Trim back the 45° seam allowance to 6 mm (¼ in). Turn through to the right side to form the mitre and press.

CLOSURES

Closures can be unobtrusive and hidden, or visual and decorative.

ZIPS

Zips come in a range of weights, sizes and colours, from lightweight dress zips to heavy-duty zips for jeans and jackets. In soft furnishings we use a range of zips, which can be of standard length chosen for their colour but, more often than not, we use continuous zips, which come in a roll with separate zip sliders to be fitted as required. I also like to use concealed zips, especially on decorative cushions where both sides may be used and you do not want to see the zip.

Fitting the zip slider to continuous zip

1 Cut the length of zip required with a bit to spare. Carefully open one end of the zip, approximately 3 cm (1¼ in). Cut the teeth off one side only.

2 Insert the zip slider on the toothed side, lining it up with the beginning of the teeth on the other side.

3 Make sure the short-end teeth are pushed just inside the zip slider. Holding the two fabric ends of the zip firmly in one hand, pull the zip slider down the zip to the other end.

Centred zip insertion

The centred zip is used in the backs of box cushion borders when the zip is not to be seen, i.e. when a cushion is fitted into a chair. It can also be used on the backs of scatter cushions, when the front has a clearly distinctive decorative front. The zip can run across the entire back or can be 5 cm (2 in) shorter than the finished seam.

1 Overlock the raw edges of the fabric. Machine the two pieces of fabric together along the seam allowance at one end. Then lengthen the machine stitch and place a temporary machine stitch the length of the zip. Reduce the stitch length again and machine stitch the seam allowance at the other end. Press the seam open.

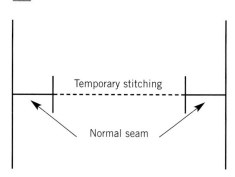

Temporary stitching

Normal seam

2 With wrong sides facing, place the teeth of the zip on the temporary seam line. Pin and/or tack in place.

3 With right sides facing and starting from the bottom of the zip, machine stitch across the bottom of the zip; turn and machine the length of the zip, finishing at the top of the zip. When you reach the slider, lift the presser foot and move the slider down the zip out of the way, then continue to machine stitch the zip in place.

4 Starting from the bottom of the zip again, machine stitch down the other side of the zip, finishing across the top of the zip. Take out the temporary stitches.

TIP Always machine in the same direction down each side of a zip. This will stop distortion, which can happen if you machine around the zip in one direction only.

Concealed zip insertion

Concealed zips are ideal for lightweight and striped fabrics as the zips can be completely hidden.

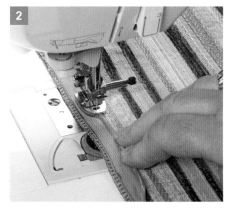

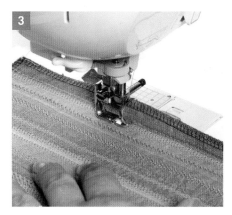

1 Overlock the raw edges of the fabric. Open the zip. With wrong sides of the zip facing, pin the zip to the right side of the fabric. Using the zip foot, machine stitch the zip as close to the outside edge of the fabric as possible.

2 Now fit the concealed zip foot to the machine and machine stitch as close to the teeth as possible, holding the zip teeth flat as you stitch.

3 Close the zip. Machine stitch the seam closed at each end of the zip.

Lapped zip insertion into a piped scatter cushion

This is the most popular form of zip insertion into a cushion cover.

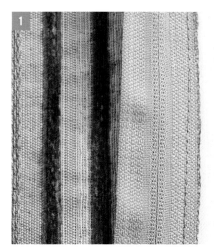

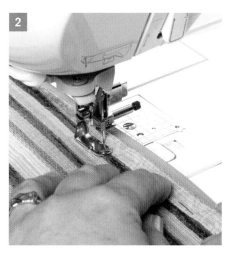

1 Overlock all the raw edges of the fabric. Make up and attach the piping to the front of the cushion. See Piping on pages 52–3. With right sides together, machine stitch the zip to the outside edge of the un-piped back fabric.

2 Fold the fabric over the zip teeth and, using the zip foot, stitch in place close to the teeth.

3 Attach the zip to the piped side. Position the zip teeth as close as possible to the piping and stitch in place.

4 Open the zip slightly. Pin the two cushion pieces together and stitch in place around the other three sides and 2 cm (¾ in) in at each end of the zip. Open the zip fully and turn through to the right side.

FASTENINGS

You may find the following fastenings useful on various projects. Some are designed to be hidden whilst others are more decorative and are used for display.

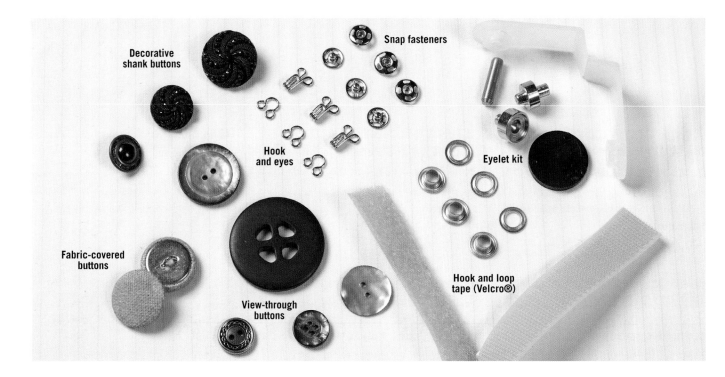

Decorative shank buttons

Snap fasteners

Hook and eyes

Eyelet kit

Fabric-covered buttons

View-through buttons

Hook and loop tape (Velcro®)

BUTTONS

Buttons come in a range of shapes and sizes. They can be plain or highly decorative, or can be covered in fabric. There are two basic types of button:
- View-through, with two or four holes for attaching.
- Shank, meaning it has either a metal, plastic or fabric shank behind the button for attaching.

If you wish to cover buttons in fabric, this can be done quite easily with a simple buttoning kit, but if you want a button to hold tension, then it will need to be made on a buttoning machine, as kit buttons often pop under tension.

FABRIC TIES

Fabric ties can be any length or width, and you may need to experiment to get the desired effect.

1 **Cut strips of fabric four times the finished width of the tie required by the required length. Fold the raw edges in towards the centre.**

2 **Fold the strip in half lengthways, and machine stitch as close as possible to the edge and across the ends.**

HOOK AND LOOP TAPE (VELCRO®)

Velcro consists of two strips of fabric. The hook strip has tiny hooks that will intermesh when pressed onto the soft loop strip. The soft side should always be fitted to the soft furnishings (to the top of a blind for instance) and the hook side fitted to the track systems. This way, when the blind is washed or cleaned it will not get hooked up on anything else.

PASSEMENTERIE

Passementerie is the art of decorative tassels and trimmings. Today we still see trimmings on the trappings of royal, military and civic regalia, as well as in interior designs to embellish window curtains and blinds, as well as beds and upholstered furniture.

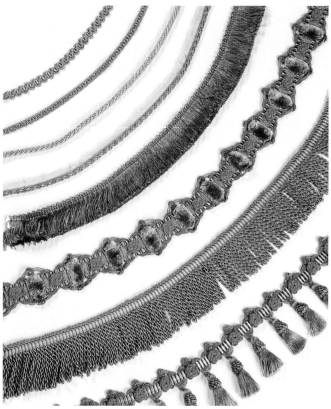

TASSELS

Today, tassels are made from a miriad of threads, fibres, ribbons and feathers, enhanced with beading and decorative suspension cords. Large or small, simple or adorned with decorative detailing, they are used to decorate curtain holdbacks, drapery, cushions, key fobs and furniture.

BRAIDS

There is a huge array of braids that can be applied to soft furnishings, from the simple to most intricate: flat, ruched, fringes, skirts, tassels, beading and a combination of all. Braids are hand-stitched to curtains, blinds, drapes, bedding, cushions, chairs and sofas.

GIMP

Gimp is a decorative braid that is woven in scroll formation that allows it to follow the curves of furnishings: headboards, pelmets, cushions and furniture.

CORDS

Decorative cords are stitched to top fabrics by hand. You will need to use a strong thread and a small stitch at the back of the cord.

Flanged cords are attached to a piece of tape that is stitched into a seam. Although quicker to attach, flanged cords are less effective as you can never hide the flange completely.

JOINING FLANGED CORDS

1 Stitch the cord to one side of the cushion cover, as close to the cord as possible, leaving a 3 cm (1¼ in) gap between the two ends.

2 Undo the flange from the cord, back to the stitching on each side and cross the two pieces of flange and machine together.

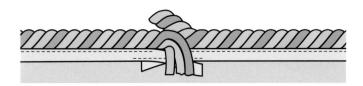

3 Untwist the cords a little at one end and flatten the strands.

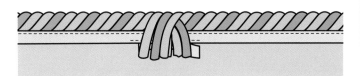

4 Untwist the cords a little at the other end and flatten these strands over the first strands.

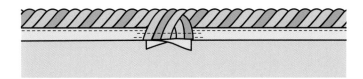

5 Machine stitch over all the strands and cut off any excess.

Note: It is not always possible to keep the different coloured twists in the same order.

PIPING

Piping is a fixed decorative treatment that is sewn into a seam. Piping can be self-piping using the same fabric, or can be covered in a contrast fabric for a more distinctive effect.

TIP If you only have natural piping cord and you need to use it on something that may need to be washed, you can pre-shrink it yourself. Pour boiling water over the cord to shrink it and then dry it before using. Remember to cut more than you actually require to allow for the shrinkage.

Piping fabric should be cut on the true cross, which will enable the piping to twist and curve around shapes more easily. However, in soft furnishings, in order to cut costs and to make the most effective use of fabrics, it is acceptable to cut piping fabric on as sharp an angle as possible.

TIP If you are using a fine fabric and don't want to see the twist in the cord through it, you can either double up the thickness of the fabric or line the fabric with a piece of lining fabric.

Single piping
Piping fabric that is cut 4 cm (1½ in) wide will give you a seam allowance of 1.5 cm (⅝ in) once it has been made up.

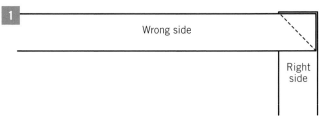

1 Cut strips of fabric, on the cross, at least 4 cm (1½ in) wide. With right sides of the fabric together, and the fabric's pile/pattern running in the same direction, sew along the diagonal. Join all the strips together, trim back the seams to 6 mm (¼ in) and open out flat.

2 Place the piping cord in the centre of the strip of fabric. Fold the fabric over so that the raw edges are equal and, using a piping foot or zipper foot, stitch in place.

Joining piping

Joins in piping that are made on the cross are less obtrusive. Always join piping on the side of a piece of work, never on the front edge or at corners.

1 To join two end of piping together, attach the piping to the fabric leaving 10 cm (4 in) free at each end. Cut one end of the piping off square. Lay the other end of the piping over this piece, measure a 4 cm (1½ in) overlap, and cut off the excess. You should now have a 4 cm (1½ in) overlap. Unpick the piping at each end, back to the stitching.

2 With right sides of the fabric together and at right angles to each other, join the piping fabric together, stitching along the diagonal.

TIP At this point, pull the piping fabric flat to make sure that you have stitched across the diagonal in the right direction. If it will not lie flat, you have stitched the wrong angle.

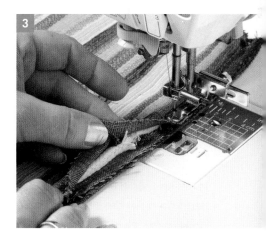

3 Once you are happy that you have stitched in the right direction, trim back the seam allowance and open out flat. Cut the two pieces of piping cord so that they butt together nicely. Place back under the machine's foot and stitch in place.

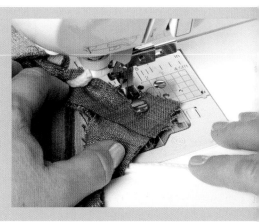

TIP This joining method will always work if you remember that the overlap must always be the same as the width of the piping fabric. So, if you are using a different sized piping cord and need to adjust the width of the piping fabric, make sure you use this same measurement for the overlap at the join.

DECORATIVE TECHNIQUES

Learning a few basic decorative techniques will help you turn your designs into something special. You don't have to go all out with decorative detail, but learning to combine some basic techniques with fabrics and trimmings will give your work the 'wow' factor. Do not be afraid to experiment.

TIP With any decorative technique it is always advisable to sample the technique first. Fabrics react differently depending on their thickness and quality. What may look great in one fabric may look miserable in another. Also, fabric quantities can vary quite dramatically. If you have sampled the technique first, you will be sure it is right for your design and that you have the correct amount of fabric.

GATHERING FABRIC

I find this method of gathering fabric to be the easiest:

1 Fold the frill fabric in half, right sides together, and machine stitch the ends. Turn the fabric through to the right sides and press. Use a strong thread as long as the frill fabric and anchor it at one end of the fabric. Do not be temped to cut off a length of thread, as you only need its full length until you have pulled up the gathers, otherwise you will be wasting a lot of thread unnecessarily.

2 Extend the machine's zigzag stitch as long and as wide as possible, and machine stitch over the thread.

3 Holding the strong thread taught, push the fabric up on the thread to the required length of the frill. Ease out the gathers evenly and pin to the body of your fabric.

4 Then sew the gathered frill to the fabric using a holding stitch 1 cm (⅜ in) in from the raw edge. Make sure all gathering stitches are enclosed within the seam allowances.

FRILLS

Frills don't have to be flimsy and frilly; combined with other fabrics they can be quite substantial and effective. A drop-down frill with a contrast edge on a long pair of curtains can make very plain curtains into something special. Frills can be made using the same or contrasting fabrics. They can be singular or layered up using different types of fabric to create a whole array of effects. Puffed headings and ruched borders are just slight variations on a frill.

The basic frill is created by gathering up the fabric. To create a good frill you will need 2 to 2.5 times the finished length required by twice the depth required, plus seam allowances.

TIP When working on very long lengths of frill, it is better to divide the frill into smaller manageable sections, which you then match to a similar number of sections on the main fabric. This will make sure the gathers are evenly distributed, i.e. into four equal sections, one for each side of a cushion.

PLEATS

Pleats are a more formal way of gathering fabric. They can be used for decorative purposes in the manipulation of the fabrics before they are used on different projects, such as decorative pleats within panels of fabric on cushions or bedding. Or they can form a more practical application on chair skirts and bed valances, where one end of the pleat is left hanging free to allow movement.

There are three basic pleat formations:

KNIFE PLEATS

Knife pleats can be spaced or touching, but all the pleats face in one direction.

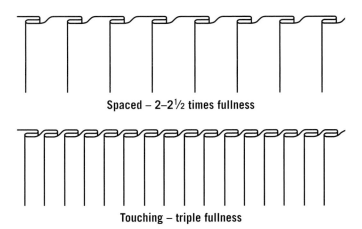

Spaced – 2–2½ times fullness

Touching – triple fullness

BOX PLEATS

Box pleats can also be spaced or touching, as above.

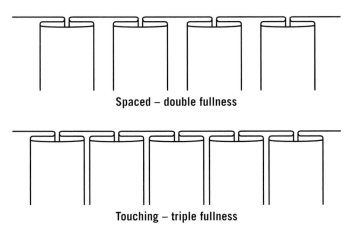

Spaced – double fullness

Touching – triple fullness

KICK PLEATS

Kick pleats are folds of pleated fabric, usually found at corners. They can be made in two ways:

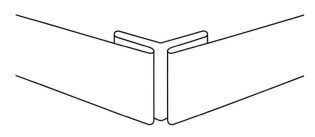

Allow an additional 40 cm (16 in) for the pleat.

- To form a pleat that is completely enclosed, you will need four times the amount of fabric required for the pleat, i.e. an extra 40 cm (16 in). If you want to use a contrast fabric for the pleat, the seams should be placed on the inside fold of the pleat.

- Alternatively, you can make a dummy kick pleat, where the pleat is a separate piece of fabric. This is particularly useful if you want movement in the skirt, such as on the side of a bed valance to enable you to lift the skirt out of the way to allow access to drawers in a divan bed.

PLEAT FABRIC ALLOWANCES

The size and number of pleats required will vary depending on the size and style of the project you are working on. You may need to experiment to see which effect you prefer and to calculate the amount of fabric required.

Type of pleat	Fullness required
Knife pleat – touching	x 3
Knife pleat – spaced	x 2–2.5
Box pleat – touching	x 3
Box pleat – spaced	x 2–2.25
Kick pleat	+ 40 cm (16 in)

TOUCHING KNIFE PLEATS

You will need three times the length of fabric required by twice the depth, plus seam allowances.

1 With right sides together, fold the fabric in half lengthways. Machine stitch the two ends closed. Turn through to the right side and press flat. Mark the top edge every 2.5 cm (1 in). Fold the fabric so that the third mark touches the first mark, and pin in place. Move to the sixth mark and fold the fabric so that it touches the fourth mark, and pin in place. Fold the fabric at the ninth mark so that it touches the seventh mark, and pin in place. Repeat this process for the length of the fabric. Press the pleats in place.

2 Attach the pleats to the main fabric, right sides together. Machine the pleats in place 1 cm (⅜ in) from the raw edge. **Note:** Spaced knife pleats have a gap between each pleat.

BOX PLEATS

Box pleats fold back on themselves with folds on either side. They can be spaced or touching. Always experiment with the pleat spacing in order to calculate the fabric requirements and the desired effect.

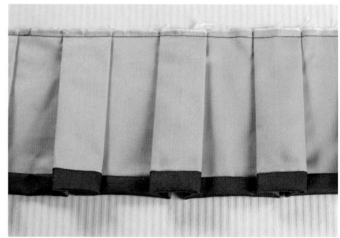

5 cm (2 in) box pleats spaced 2.5 cm (1 in) apart are formed by marking every 2.5 cm (1 in) along the top edge of the fabric. Fold back on the first mark and place at the back of the second mark and pin in place. Fold back the third mark and pin to the fifth mark and pin in place. Fold back at the eighth mark and pin to the sixth mark. Fold back on the tenth mark and pin to the twelfth mark. Continue in this way to the end of the fabric.

TUCKS

Tucks are another form of fabric manipulation. The size and spacing of tucks can vary to form many different effects. Larger tucks can also be pushed in different directions to form wave effects.

PIN TUCKS

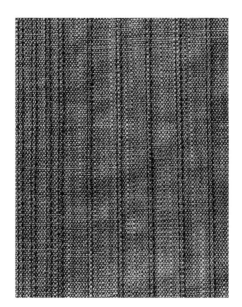

Pin tucks are created by using a twin needle and a pin tuck foot attachment. If you wish to use a cord to enhance the effect, the pin tuck foot has grooves on the underside that will help guide fine cord. Make sure the twin needle and the pin tuck foot are the correct size.

When threading the machine for a twin needle, you will need two reels of thread. Most machines will allow for two spools of thread to be used at a time. Do not twist the threads together when threading the machine as they need to move freely. Often you will find a thread guide on either side of the presser foot shank to accommodate a thread either side. Your threads must be of equal weight or the work will become unbalanced.

1 Increase the tension on the top thread slightly to make the pin tucks more pronounced.

2 Place the fabric completely under the presser foot and, stitching quite slowly, machine stitch down the length of the fabric. If you want to use a cord to enhance the look of the pin tucks, place the cord under the fabric and between the grooves of the foot. Make sure you keep the cord in the centre of the groove as you machine down the length of the fabric. Hold the end of the cord as you start to sew.

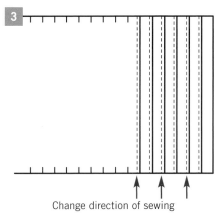

Change direction of sewing

3 To help avoid distortion, turn the fabric and now work in the opposite direction.

4 Line the foot up with the previous tuck and machine stitch the next row. Continue as required.

MINI TUCKS

Mini tucks are very narrow folds forming fine lines of texture in fabric. They can be made quite easily by using an edging foot or with a zip foot on your sewing machine.

1 Working from the centre out, fold and press the fabric down the centre and position the machine's foot close to the edge of the fabric.

2 Machine stitch down the length of the fabric, keeping the foot in line with the fold at all times.

3 Re-fold the fabric the required distance apart and machine down the length of the fold line, this time machining in the opposite direction to avoid distortion. Repeat as required.

CROSS TUCKS

WAVE TUCKS

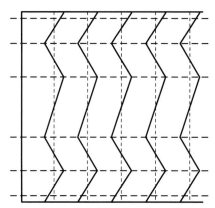

You can also turn the fabric and work mini tucks across the fabric in the same way. Make sure that when you cross a mini tuck you always push all the folds in the same direction.

Alternatively, wider tucks can be pushed in waves by alternating the direction of the folds at regular intervals across the width.

RUCHED FABRIC EFFECTS

Ruched fabric is a variation on gathering. Ruched fabrics can be inset into panels of fabric or used to create ruched borders and piping.

RUCHED BORDERS

Ruched borders look very effective when padded on the borders of cushions and bed throws.

Ruched and wadded border
Fabric requirements: 2 to 2.5 times the total length of the border by twice the depth of the border, plus seam allowances. Do not forget you need a seam allowance on both sides of the border fabric.

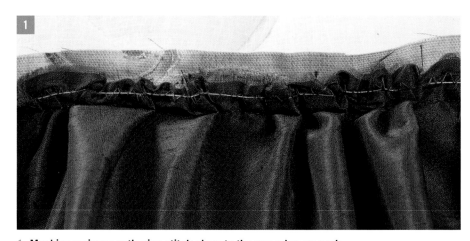

1 Machine a zigzag gathering stitch close to the raw edge on each side of the border fabric. See Gathering fabric on page 54. Pull the gathers up on one side and, with right sides together, attach to the body of the fabric.

2 Pull up the gathers evenly on the other side of the border fabric. Inset a roll of polyester wadding. Fold the ruched border fabric over the wadding and herringbone stitch to the seam allowance only.

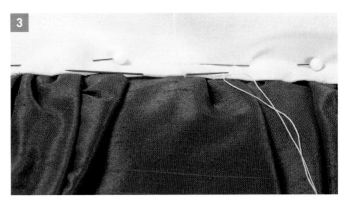

3 For a bed throw, use the lining fabric to cover all the raw edges and slip stitch in place.

Ruched borders look very effective when padded on the borders of cushions and bed throws.

Alternatively, you can insert the border into a seam, as with cushions:

1 Attach the ruched border fabric to one side of the cushion cover. Pull up the gathers on the other side of the border fabric and insert a roll of polyester wadding. Fold the border fabric over the wadding and pin in place.

2 Attach the back of the cushion cover and machine stitch in place, enclosing all raw edges and gathering stitches within the seam allowance. Turn the cushion cover through to the right side.

TIP Make sure you have tight gathers at the corners, so that once the cushion is turned through to the right sides of the fabric, the gathers will be evenly distributed both sides of the corners.

RUCHED PIPING

Ruched piping is another very effective decorative detail. It can be particularly effective on cushions.

1 Cut piping fabric 6 cm (2½ in) wide. Insert the piping cord into the centre of the piping fabric and, with raw edges together, machine stitch in place 1 cm (⅜ in) from the raw edges.

2 Ruche the fabric up on the piping cord to the finished length required. Insert into a seam as normal.

TIP With ruched piping, don't be tempted to cut off a length of piping cord as you only need the full length whilst sewing it into the piping fabric. Once pushed up on the cord, you only need half the original amount of cord.

RUCHED FABRIC STRIPS

Ruched fabric strips can be inserted into panels of plain ungathered fabric.

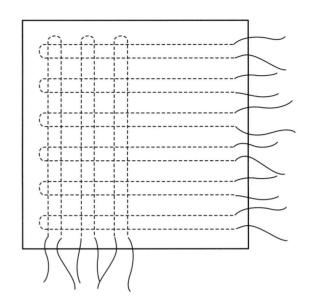

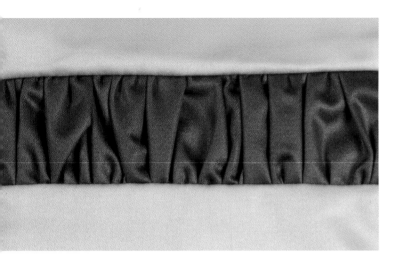

RUCHED FABRIC PANELS

A panel of ruched fabric can also be formed but must be surrounded with a plain border to make it look most effective.

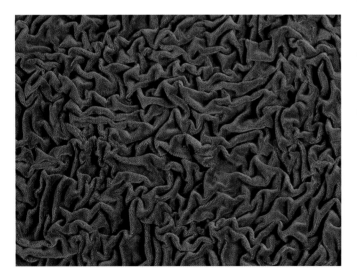

Fabric requirements: you will need up to four times the amount of fabric for this technique. However, I suggest you sample a piece first to be sure. This technique can be done on the sewing machine, but I find the best results are achieved by hand.

1 Cut a large square of fabric. Using a long sewing machine stitch length or a large running stitch, follow the pattern shown in the diagram above. Use one continuous length of thread for each up and down row, spaced approximately 1 cm (⅜ in) apart. Make sure you form a 'U' shape at one end of each row.

2 Once you have worked from one side of the fabric to the other, turn the fabric 90° and do the same again across the fabric.

3 Holding the fabric firmly, pull up all the threads, one side at a time. Arrange the gathers into an evenly-distributed pleasing form. Secure the ends of the threads to stop them coming unravelled. For best effect, fit a plain border around the ruched fabric.

Ruched fabric can be used to form decorative panels on:
• Cushions
• Blinds
• Bed throws
• Pelmets
• Tiebacks
• Borders

LATTICE OR CANADIAN SMOCKING

Lattice smocking is a beautiful way of giving fabric texture. Un-crushable materials such as velvet, corduroy, satin and heavy furnishing fabrics are all suitable and will produce interesting and rich effects, but it can also be done with fine silks.

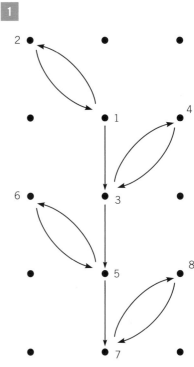

If you want to enhance the padded effect on fine fabrics, you can add a small piece of polyester wadding behind each stitch. Whatever you do, it is a good idea to sample a piece first. This will not only confirm the visual effect, but by working a small measured sample, it will enable you to calculate the amount of fabric required. Lattice smocking reduces by about 50 per cent, but by working a sized sample you will be able to increase the fabric dimensions accordingly.

1 **Lattice smocking is worked from the wrong side of the fabric. Mark out a grid of squares, with dots placed at 2.5 cm (1 in) intervals on the back of the fabric (see template, above right).**

2 **Use a strong thread and make a knot in the end. Starting in the top left-hand corner of the fabric, pick up Dot 1 and make a small stitch.**

3 **Pick up Dot 2 and then go back to Dot 1 and pick up this stitch again.**

4 **Pull Dots 1 and 2 together and make a stitch to secure it.**

5 **Keeping the fabric and thread between Dots 1 and 3 completely flat, pick up Dot 3 and make a securing stitch.**

6 **Pick up Dot 4, then Dot 3, pull together and make a stitch.**

7 **Pick up Dot 5, and keeping the fabric and thread between Dots 3 and 5 completely flat, make a securing stitch. Repeat this process to the end of the row.**

8 **Work the next row in the same way, starting one dot down from the top.**

APPLIQUÉ

Appliqué is the positioning of small pieces of fabric that have been cut into decorative shapes and then stitched to a background fabric. The appliqué fabric pieces are attached to the main fabric and then a satin stitch or other decorative stitch is used to neaten the raw edges.

MACHINE APPLIQUÉ

The easiest way to machine appliqué is to cut out the decorative shapes using Bondaweb.

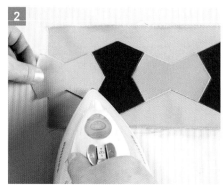

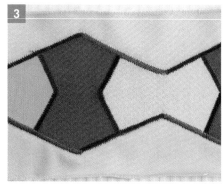

1 Make templates of your design pieces and trace or draw them, in reverse, onto a piece of Bondaweb. Iron the Bondaweb onto the wrong side of the fabric. Cut out the designs and peel off the paper backing.

2 Arrange the appliqué designs on the main fabric and iron into position.

3 Set the stitch width selector to create a satin stitch (a very small tight zigzag stitch) and stitch around the appliqué pieces, stitching them into place.

TRADITIONAL HAND APPLIQUÉ

Alternatively, you can hand-stitch appliqué pieces.

1 Draw your design onto paper. Trace the shapes and make templates of each shape out of card. Alternatively, you can use the motifs from different fabrics.

2 Lay the templates onto the fabric, right side up, and draw around them with a pencil or fabric marker pen.

3 Cut out the shapes with a 6 mm (¼ in) seam allowance all round.

4 Turn the raw edges under on the marked line, clipping the curves and corners, and tack close to the edge. Position the pieces on the main the fabric. Pin and/or tack in place.

5 Stitch the appliquéd designs down using a very small slip stitch or other decorative stitch, removing the tacking stitches as you go.

PATCHWORK

Patchwork is another of those traditional sewing skills, often used when sewing together treasured pieces of precious fabric in, sometimes, very complicated designs. Patchwork can be sewn by hand or by machine. The patchwork designs can be very basic geometric shapes or can have very complicated and intricate designs. The choice is yours, but with a few pieces of fabric and some very basic design ideas you can create individual one-off designs that will enhance a room scheme and can be treasured for many years to come.

PATCHWORK DESIGNS

Patchwork designs can be very simple geometric designs or random shapes, through to the more complex folding of fabric into a star formation.

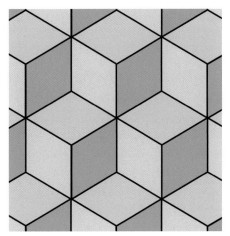

Geometric

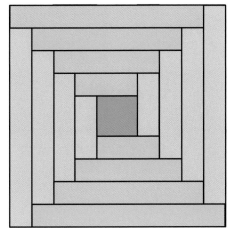

Log cabin

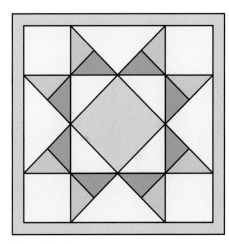

Repeat blocks

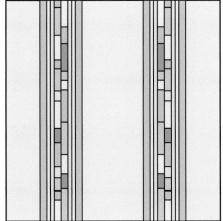

Strip patchwork

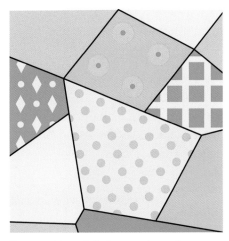

Crazy patchwork (using precious pieces of fabric)

Folded star

BLOCK AND STRIP PATCHWORK

Block or strip patchwork is probably the simplest patchwork to create, but by mixing fabrics, can be most effective.

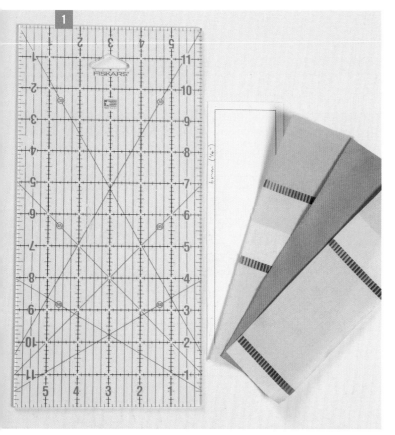

1 Make templates of any shapes required. Make sure you include a 6 mm (¼ in) seam allowance all round. Mark out the fabrics using a fine pencil or quilter's pencil.

2 Cut out the fabrics using scissors or, for long, straight edges, you can use a rotary cutter. Store the various pieces of fabric appropriately.

3 Pin the smaller pieces into strips and machine stitch in place using a 6 mm (¼ in) seam allowance. Press the seam allowances flat.

4 Making sure the seams are aligned, pin together and machine stitch the larger blocks or strips, using a 6 mm (¼ in) seam allowance, to form your completed panel. Press the seams flat.

5 Once you have completed the patchwork panel, you can then enhance the design with beading, embroidery stitches, topstitching, etc.

The panel is now ready to be made up into your chosen project:
• Bed throws/quilts
• Cushions
• Pelmets
• Tiebacks

QUILTING

Quilting soft furnishings has been around for centuries. It is an old, traditional decorative technique. The art of building up layers of fabric with decorative stitching to hold them in place is ideal for bedspreads. By trapping air between the layers, the quilt's thermal insulating properties are increased.

QUILTING DESIGNS

Designs do not have to be complicated. Often the simplest of designs is most effective. If you intend to machine quilt, look for designs that can be stitched in a continuous motion.

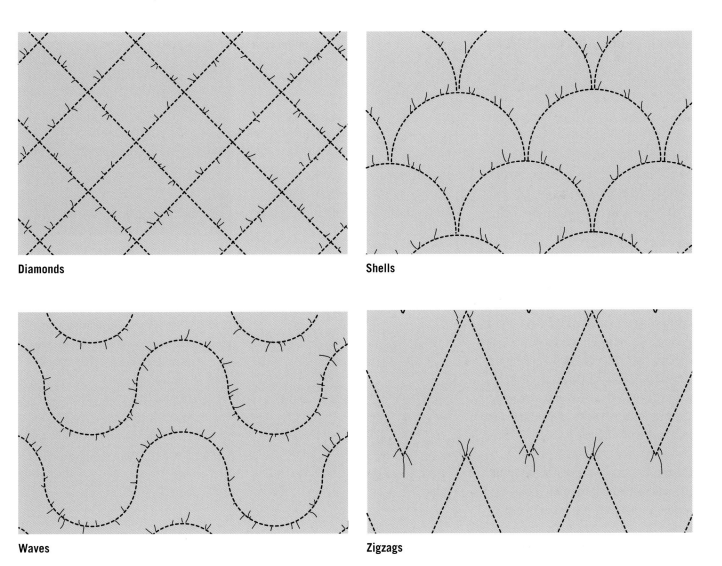

Diamonds

Shells

Waves

Zigzags

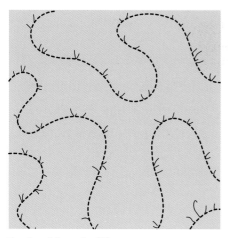

Freehand (vermicelli)

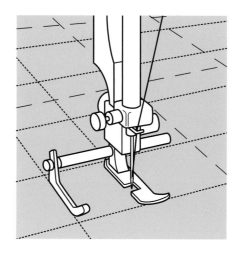

Curved line quilting

MARKING OUT QUILTING DESIGNS

The marking out of designs, other than the following of seam lines or patterns, should be done before the quilt is layered together. There is a variety of marking tools available: 3H pencils, silver and yellow quilter's pencils, washable marking pens, etc. Whichever you choose, always test the marker on a scrap of the fabric first. You should be able to remove any marks after you have quilted it.

Quilting, particularly machine quilting, will reduce the size of the fabrics, so it is advisable to make the quilting slightly larger to allow for this. Always sample a piece of quilting in order to work out how much bigger it should be and to allow for the correct tension of the stitch. In general, the stitch length needs to be longer than for regular sewing. It is also advisable, but not essential, to use a backing fabric as some sewing machines require a backing fabric under the polyester wadding to stop it catching in the dog-feed;

muslin, thin cotton, calico or lining fabrics can all be used. The backing and wadding should be slightly bigger than the quilt top. Once the quilting has been finished, it can then be cut to size and finished as appropriate.

A walking foot or even-feed foot machine is essential when quilting to prevent tucks forming in the quilt top or backing.

Working with an adjustable gauge will help you keep the same distance apart when working lines or grid effects.

LAYERING THE QUILT

You will need to layer up your fabrics and hold them together firmly before you start stitching.

1 Lay out the backing fabric, right side down, smooth out and stretch taut.

2 Lay the wadding (preferably 4-oz polyester wadding) on the top of the backing and the quilt fabric on top of the wadding, with right side up. Pin the layers together, working from the centre out.

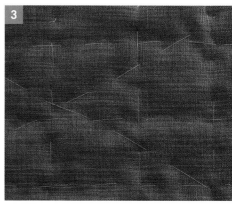

3 Baste the layers together. This can be done with thread or safety pins. When using thread, take long pieces of thread, start in the middle and baste to the outer edge in rows in all directions. When using safety pins, these should be placed all over the quilt at intervals no greater than a hand's width in any one direction.

Alternatively, you can use short plastic tags that can be shot through the quilt with a basting tag gun.

MACHINE QUILTING

Machine quilting large pieces can be very difficult when using a domestic sewing machine. Therefore, it is best to work small panels that can then be joined together.

1 Roll the quilt fabric as tight as possible to the middle. Start machine stitching working from the middle, out. Support the fabric at all times or you will break the machine's needle.

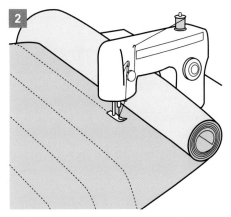

2 Work continuously in rows or follow the marked design.

3 Once you have worked to the outside edge, turn the fabric around and roll the other edge tightly to the centre. Continue to stitch the other side in the same way.

Alternatively, there are specialist quilting companies that will do the larger pieces for you that you can then finish off

Outline quilting using a chain stitch industrial sewing machine.

DECORATIVE EDGES

The edges of valances, skirts, roman blinds, curtain leading edges and cushions can all incorporate a shaped edge: scalloped, pointed and curved, to name but a few. They can be created in the main fabric or can be made with a contrast fabric that is then attached to the main fabric. Whichever you decide to do, you must first work on the shape and design of the edge.

SHAPED EDGES

In order to get a good, neat finish, it is best to produce the shaped edge with a facing, ideally in the same fabric. This is particularly important when working with sharp angles.

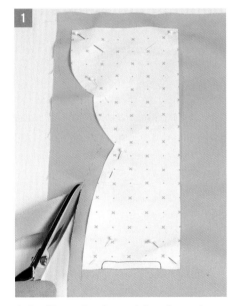

1 Decide on the shape of the edge and make a paper pattern. Working from the centre, draw one half of the shaped edge on a piece of paper and then mirror image the shape from the centre for the other half. Make a paper pattern, adding a 1.5 cm (½ in) seam allowance. Place the paper pattern on the fabric and mark out the position of the shape with a pencil or marker pen. Cut out along this line.

2 Mark out the shape on the facing fabric in the same way. The facing fabric should be the depth of the shaped edge plus a seam allowance. If you are making a roman blind, add an extra 10 cm (4 in) to create a double 5 cm (2 in) hem for the bottom weight of the blind.

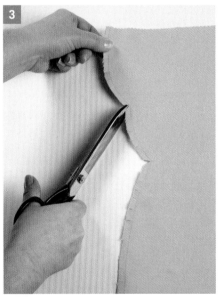

3 With right sides together, pin the shaped facing fabric to the main fabric and machine stitch along the bottom shaped edge, with a 1.5 cm (⅝ in) seam allowance. Trim, snip and notch the seam allowance around any curves to ease the fabric when turning through.

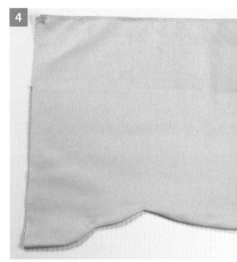

4 Turn through to the right side of the fabric and iron in place. Insert into the seams of cushions or finish making blinds in the usual way.

This method can also be used for creating shapes on the borders of curtains and cushions, bedding and skirts, and angles on pelmets. You just need to pay heed to the depth of the facing.

DOG TOOTH DECORATIVE EDGE ON A BLIND

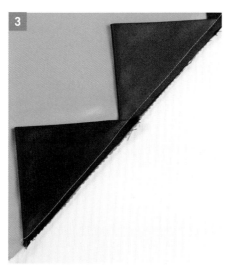

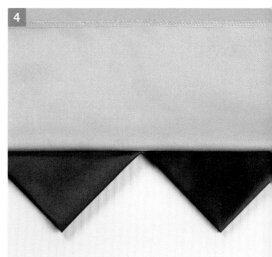

1 Cut 18 cm (7 in) squares of a contrast fabric. Fold in half on the diagonal and then in half again. With a 1.5 cm (5⁄8 in) seam allowance, this will give you a triangle of fabric approximately 7.5 cm (3 in) deep.

2 Cut a strip of the main fabric the width of the blind by 12 cm (4½ in) deep, to use as the facing.

3 With right sides together, fit the triangles along the bottom edge of the blind. Make sure that you start and stop the triangles 2 cm (¾ in) in from each edge, so that when you turn the sides in they will be lined up with the outside edge of the blind. Check that the triangles are lined up and correctly spaced. The spacing of the triangles can be adjusted by inserting each inside the fold of its neighbour. Machine stitch in place 1 cm (⅜ in) from the raw edge.

4 With right sides together, place the facing fabric on top of the triangles and machine stitch in place with a 1.5 cm (5⁄8 in) seam allowance.

TIP Any decorative shape or trimming can be applied in the same way. See Roman blind project on pages 133–35. For a cushion, insert the dog tooth triangles between the front and back cushion pieces.

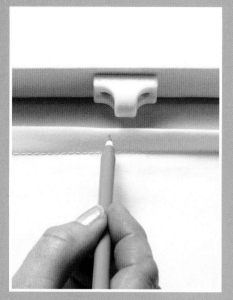 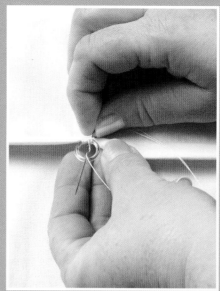 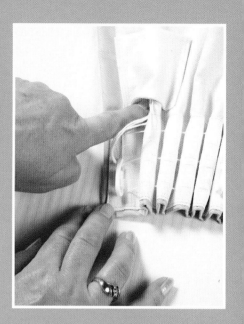

BASICS

STANDARD ROMAN BLINDS

Roman blinds are a popular window treatment that give a contemporary feel to any room scheme.

They hang flat when let down to their full length, and in horizontal pleats of approximately 15 to 30 cm (6 to 12 in) deep when pulled up. They can be fitted either inside or outside the window recess. Roman blinds cover part of the window, so if light is an issue, it should be remembered that this type of blind takes up even more window. Therefore, they are best suited to tall windows or windows that have a large amount of space above them, where the blind can be fitted without covering too much of the window itself. Roman blinds can be unlined, lined or interlined with a lightweight domette.

1 If you are going to do any decorative techniques on your blind, such as borders, appliqué, inset panels, braids and trimmings, you will need to do these before you make the blind. See Decorative techniques on pages 54–69.

2 Once you have chosen the design and decided whether the blind will hang inside or outside the window recess, take accurate measurements of your window and complete the measuring chart (see page 39).

TIP When measuring your window, take three measurements each way: top, middle and bottom, as well as left, right and centre. Windows are rarely true, so use the smaller of these measurements, particularly if the blind is to be fitted inside the recess.

3 Choose your mode of fixing: wooden batten or track system.

4 Calculate the fabric requirements:
Main fabric: measure the finished drop and width of the blind and
– Add 20 cm (8 in) for the hem and top allowances
– Add 8 cm (3¼ in) to the finished width
– If the blind is wider than one width of fabric, you will need twice as much fabric, plus any pattern repeat. See Pattern matching on pages 35–7.

Lining fabric: allow an extra 3 or 4 cm (1¼ or 1½ in) for each rod pocket and
– Add an extra 2 cm (¾ in) to the finished width of the blind

TIP You will need to allow 3 cm (1¼ in) for rod pockets with rings or 4 cm (1½ in) for rod pockets made with eyelets.

5 Now calculate the pleat dimensions. Remember, each pleat has a front and a back, except the bottom pleat which only has a front i.e. 3 rods = 7 half-pleats, 4 rods = 9 half-pleats.

6 Measure the distance from the top of the track/batten system to the bottom of the cord guides.

7 Deduct this measurement from the finished drop of the blind to give you the amount of fabric for the pleats.

8 Divide this figure by the number of half-pleats required (this will always be an odd number as the last pleat only has a front).

9 This will give you the depth of each half pleat. See example calculations, opposite.

STANDARD ROMAN BLIND PLEAT CALCULATIONS

Example: 70 cm (27½ in) wide x 132 cm (52 in) drop

132 cm (52 in) blind drop
- 6 cm (3 in) track/batten allowance

---

126 cm (49 in) divided by 7 (3 whole pleats + 1 half-pleat = 7 half-pleats) = 18 cm (7 in)

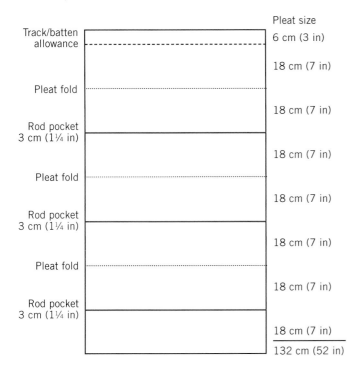

	Pleat size
Track/batten allowance	6 cm (3 in)
	18 cm (7 in)
Pleat fold	
	18 cm (7 in)
Rod pocket 3 cm (1¼ in)	
	18 cm (7 in)
Pleat fold	
	18 cm (7 in)
Rod pocket 3 cm (1¼ in)	
	18 cm (7 in)
Pleat fold	
	18 cm (7 in)
Rod pocket 3 cm (1¼ in)	
	18 cm (7 in)
	132 cm (52 in)

TO MAKE

1 Cut the main fabric to size: allow an extra 20 cm (8 in) for the top and hem, and an extra 8 cm (3¼ in) wider than the finished width of the blind.

2 If the blind is wider than a width of fabric, you will need to join the fabric together, matching any pattern. Remember, any joins should be equal on either side of a full width of fabric. See Pattern matching on pages 35–7.

3 Cut the lining fabric an extra 10 cm (4 in) longer than the finished length of the blind to allow for the top and hem, plus an extra 3 cm (1¼ in) for each rod pocket (4 cm / 1½ in if using eyelets). Also, cut the lining an extra 2 cm (¾ in) wider than the finished width of the blind.

4 Lay the main fabric on the table, wrong side up, turn the sides in 4 cm (1½ in) and serge stitch in place.

5 Turn the bottom hem up a double 5 cm (2 in) and crease in the folds.

6 Now work on the lining fabric. Turn the sides in 2.5 cm (1 in) and iron in place.

7 Turn up the bottom edge, enough to hold the blind's bottom weight (i.e. 4 cm / 1½ in) and machine stitch in place, close to the raw edge.

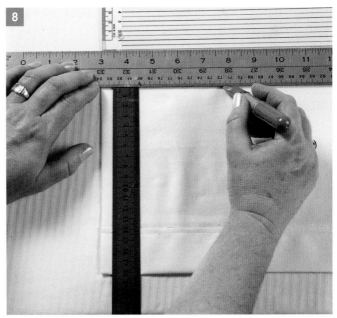

8 Measure and mark the position of the pleats and rod pockets. Work on the wrong side of the lining fabric and use a setsquare and long ruler to make sure the lines are square and parallel. Measure up from the bottom edge and, using a pencil, mark the position of the bottom of the first rod pocket.

9 **Allowing 3 cm (1¼ in) per rod pocket (4 cm/1½ in for eyelets), mark the position of the top of the rod pocket. Measure and mark the rest of the rod pockets in the same way.**

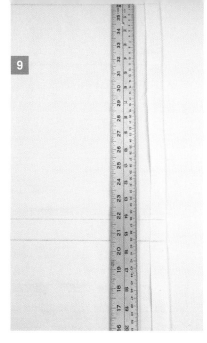

10 **Matching the pencil marks, fold the rod pocket allowance with wrong sides together.**

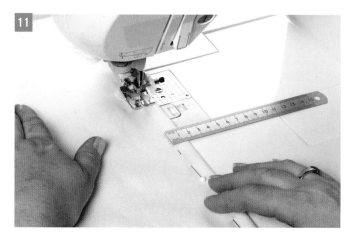

11 **Pin and machine in the rod pockets, 1.5 cm (⅝ in) from the folded edge. Continue in the same way for the remaining rod pockets.**

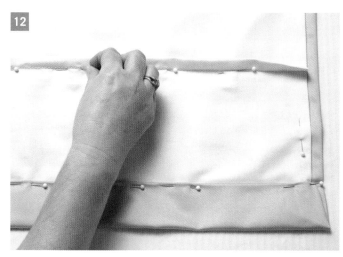

12 **With wrong sides together, place the lining on the main fabric, evenly positioned from the outside edges. Position the bottom weight pocket in the fold of the fabric that marks the bottom of the blind. Re-fold the double 5 cm (2 in) hem to enclose the weight pocket in the lining and pin in place. Quick mitre the ends so that the fabric lines up with the edge of the lining fabric. Carefully smooth the lining fabric up the blind, pinning the rod pockets in place as you go. Leave the top edge until later.**

13 **Using a 1.5 cm (⅝ in) stitch length, slip stitch the lining to the fabric, closing one end of each rod pocket as you go. Slip stitch the hem, leaving one end open to insert the bottom weight.**

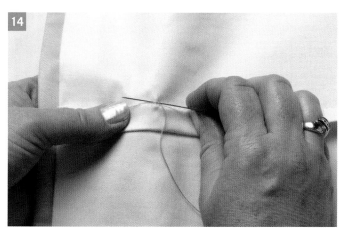

14 **Stab stitch every 30 cm (12 in) along the top edge of each rod pocket. Ideally, these stab stitches should be in line with the blind's pull cords.**

15 **Turn the fabric over with the right side up. Measure and mark the finished length of the blind with a row of pins. Attach the soft side of Velcro 6 mm (¼ in) up from this point.**

16

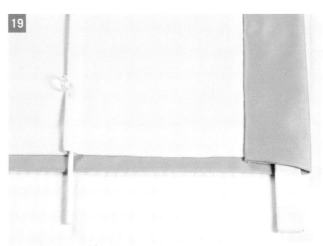

16 Turn the Velcro down on the back of the blind, and fold the raw edges under the Velcro, cutting off any excess fabric as required. Slip stitch the Velcro firmly in place.

17

17 Using the track/batten system as your guide, mark the position of the pull cords on each of the rod pockets.

18

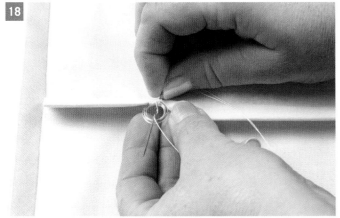

18 At these points, attach eyelets or plastic rings using a buttonhole stitch.

19

19 Cut the rods and bottom weight to length and insert into the rod and weight pockets, making sure the bottom weight goes into the pocket in the lining. Slip stitch the ends of the pockets closed.

20 Thread the pull cords through the cord guides and down through each ring, tying a slip knot on the bottom ring.

21

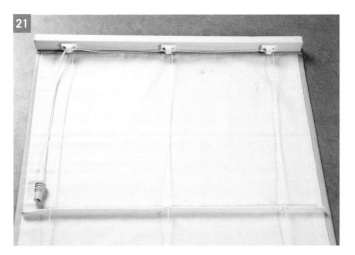

21 When all the cords are fitted, leave at least 60 cm (24 in) for the pull cord and attach a wooden acorn or brass weight. Alternatively, you can attach a cord connector at the end of the batten for a decorative pull cord. Hang and dress in your blind.

TIP If you take the rods out of the blind, you will have a soft pleated blind.

CASCADE PLEATED ROMAN BLIND

With a cascade pleated blind each pleat will hang 2.5 to 5 cm (1 to 2 in) lower than the previous one, creating a waterfall cascade effect. The construction of a cascade pleated blind is basically the same as that of a standard roman blind, you just have to calculate the pleat spacing slightly differently.

1 Decide on the number of rods required, i.e. 3 rods = 7 half-pleats.

2 Calculate the cascade and batten allowances, i.e. 5 cm (2 in) for each pleat, plus the batten allowance.

3 Deduct the cascade and batten allowances from the finished drop measurement to find the fabric allowance for the pleats.

4 Divide the fabric allowance for the pleats by the number of half-pleats to find the half-pleat size.

5 The top pleat is always two times the half-pleat size, i.e. 17.5 cm x 2 = 35 cm (7 in x 2 = 14 in).

6 Each additional whole pleat will have an extra 5 cm (2 in) added to the previous pleat (2.5 cm / 1 in for each half-pleat).

7 The bottom pleat will be half the final whole pleat allowance as it only has a front. See example calculations, opposite.

Batten allowance

Track/Batten

Pleats

Rod

Cascade allowance

Cascade allowance

Cascade allowance

CASCADE PLEATED ROMAN BLIND CALCULATIONS

Example: 70 cm (27½ in) wide x 150 cm (60 in) drop

150 cm (60 in) blind drop
- 27.5 cm (11 in) cascade and top batten allowances

122.5 cm (49 in) divided by 7 (3 whole pleats + 1 half-pleat = 7 half-pleats) = 17.5 cm (7 in)

In this example, each cascade pleat will hang 2.5 cm (1 in) below each other. Therefore, the 5 cm (2 in) cascade allowance represents 2.5 cm (1 in) for the front of the visible pleat and 2.5 cm (1 in) for the back of the visible pleat.

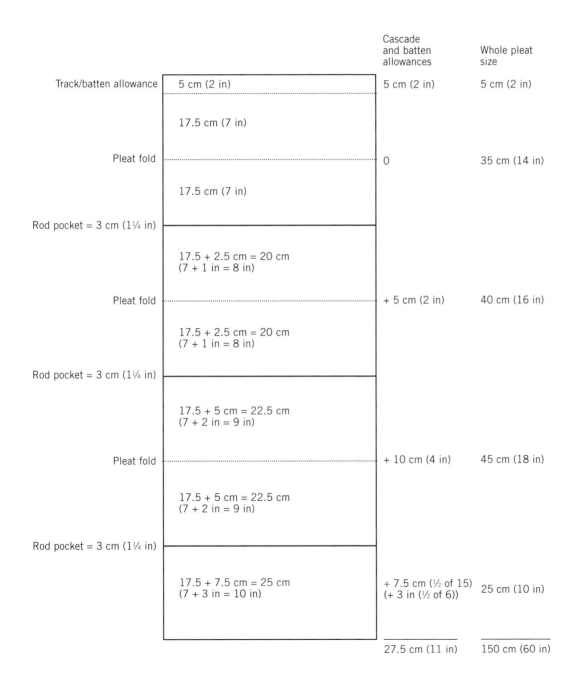

	Cascade and batten allowances	Whole pleat size
Track/batten allowance — 5 cm (2 in)	5 cm (2 in)	5 cm (2 in)
17.5 cm (7 in)		
Pleat fold	0	35 cm (14 in)
17.5 cm (7 in)		
Rod pocket = 3 cm (1¼ in)		
17.5 + 2.5 cm = 20 cm (7 + 1 in = 8 in)		
Pleat fold	+ 5 cm (2 in)	40 cm (16 in)
17.5 + 2.5 cm = 20 cm (7 + 1 in = 8 in)		
Rod pocket = 3 cm (1¼ in)		
17.5 + 5 cm = 22.5 cm (7 + 2 in = 9 in)		
Pleat fold	+ 10 cm (4 in)	45 cm (18 in)
17.5 + 5 cm = 22.5 cm (7 + 2 in = 9 in)		
Rod pocket = 3 cm (1¼ in)		
17.5 + 7.5 cm = 25 cm (7 + 3 in = 10 in)	+ 7.5 cm (½ of 15) (+ 3 in (½ of 6))	25 cm (10 in)
	27.5 cm (11 in)	150 cm (60 in)

ROLL-UP/REEF BLINDS

Roll-up or reef blinds are very simple to make, but care is needed when pulling them up. Roll-up blinds are usually made with two contrasting fabrics, as the reverse is seen when the blind is rolled up. Also, as the operating cords are seen from the front, decorative cord or ribbons can be used. These blinds will need to be fitted to a wooden batten with three small screw eyes fitted close to the front edge. You will also need a piece of dowel and a small eyelet kit.

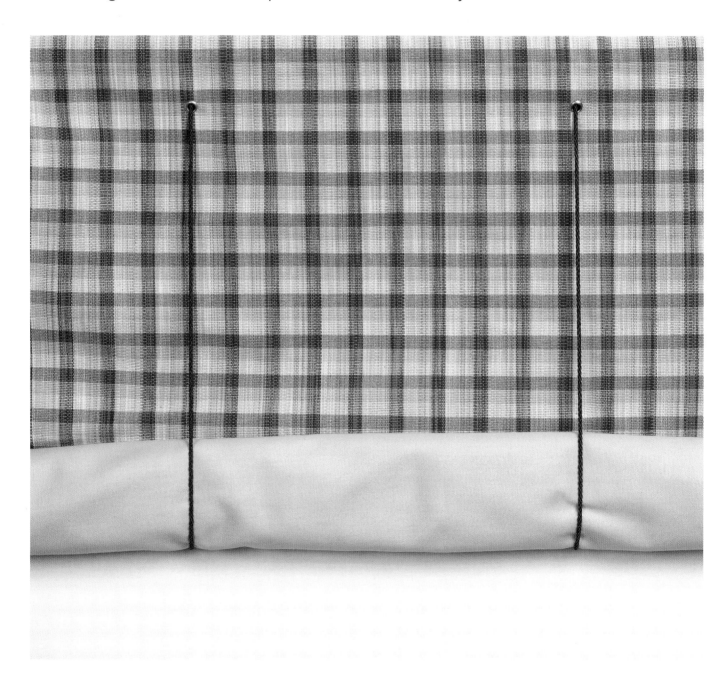

TO MAKE

1 Take accurate measurements of your window and complete the measuring chart (see page 39).

2 Measure the length of the blind required and add an extra 40 cm (16 in) to this figure for the decorative roll at the bottom.

3 Cut two pieces of fabric (front and back) the finished length of the blind plus 5 cm (2 in) for top and bottom turnings, by the finished width plus 3 cm (1¼ in) for seam allowances.

4 With right sides together and using a 1.5 cm (⅝ in) seam allowance, machine down the two sides and across the bottom edge. Turn the fabrics through to the right side and press.

5 Cut a piece of dowel 2 cm (¾ in) shorter than the finished width of the blind and drop into the bottom of the blind. Using the zip foot on your machine, stitch as close as possible to the bottom dowel to hold it in place.

6 To hold the fabrics together, and using a matching thread, stab stitch through the layers of fabric at regular intervals up the length of the blind. Space the stab stitches approximately 30 cm (12 in) apart across the width of the blind.

8 Measure the finished length of the blind and mark with a row of pins. On the right side of the fabric, attach the soft side of Velcro 6 mm (¼ in) above this point and machine stitch in place. Fold the Velcro edge down. Turn the raw edge under the Velcro and slip stitch to neaten, cutting off any excess fabric as required.

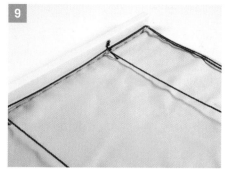

9 Cut the wooden batten 1.5 cm (⅝ in) smaller than the width of the blind and cover in lining fabric. Fit two screw eyes into the underside of the wooden batten, evenly spaced approximately 15 to 30 cm (6 to 12 in) in from each edge, depending on the width of the blind. Fit a third screw eye into the underside of the wooden batten close to the right-hand end for right-hand operation, or close to the left-hand end for left-hand operation.

10 Lining the fabric up with the batten, mark the position of the eyelets on the fabric: 5 cm (2 in) down from the top of the blind, in line with each of the two main screw eyes on the batten. Fit the eyelets according to their instructions.

11 Using two pieces of cord or ribbon, staple one end of each cord firmly behind each screw eye. Fit the blind to the batten and pass the cords down the back of the blind, up the front of the blind, through the eyelets and through the screw eyes behind them. Then pass the cords along the batten and through the third screw eye at the end.

12 Start to roll the blind and tension the cord as you go. Attach a wooden acorn to the end of the cords and tie off at a cleat on the wall.

TIP For wide blinds you may need additional cords down the centre of the blind.

CURTAINS

For me, the best looking curtains are hand-stitched, full-length interlined curtains. By adding interlining, you not only improve the thermal qualities of the curtains, but the added thickness of the interlining enhances the drape and quality of the curtain fabric, making them hang in neat folds that look full and sumptuous. The simplest curtains to make are unlined curtains with a commercial heading tape. These curtains can be hand stitched or machine made.

Whichever curtain treatment you choose you must make sure that it is in proportion to the window and the scale of the room. You can extend the visual height of a small window by fitting full-length curtains, particularly if you can utilize the space above the window as well. Alternatively, full-length curtains with swags and tails on a small window will foreshorten the room and will look over fussy and out of proportion.

When considering your window treatment, ask yourself the following questions:

- How long should the curtains be: full-length, sill-length or below the sill?
- Should they be fitted inside or outside the window recess?
- Can I use the space above the window?
- How much stack-back do I have either side of the window?
- Is there anything below the sill to hinder the fall of the curtains?
- What track or pole system is to be used?
- Is a pelmet board or fascia required?
- Are there any special requirements, i.e. for a bay window?

PROPORTIONS

- Stack-back: allow an extra 30 per cent of the window's width, or approximately 20 cm (8 in) for the stack-back.
- Curtain length:
- Full-length/sill-length: 1.5 cm (⅝ in) finished length above the floor/sill.
- Below the sill: finished length between 15–20 cm (6–8 in).

- Curtains with holdbacks or tiebacks: increase the length by 2.5–5 cm (1–2 in) to allow them to blouse out over the holder.
- Puddled curtains: allow an extra 45 cm (18 in).
- Pelmet and valance depths should be between ⅕ to ⅙ of the finished length of the curtains. The shortest part of the pelmet or valance must cover the top of the window frame.
- Tracks, poles and pelmet boards should ideally be fitted between 10–20 cm (4–8 in) above the window.

FABRIC CHOICE

When considering the fabrics to be used for a project, think not only about their colour, texture and pattern, but also think about their structure and how they will hang or drape, the length required, what linings are needed if any, headings and any other decorative details such as contrast edges or inserts, buttons or the addition of passementerie.

ESTIMATING FABRIC QUANTITIES

1 **Measure the windows and complete the measuring chart on page 39.**

2 **Choose your style of curtain:**
- **Unlined, lined or interlined**
- **Full-length, sill-length or below-sill**

3 **Choose your style of heading and calculate the fabric requirements:**

CALCULATING PLAIN FABRIC QUANTITIES

Basic formula:
Measure the width of the track or pole, and multiply by the heading fullness (see box below). Then divide by the width of the fabric = total width of fabric required.

Metric example:
Track length = 180 cm. Finished drop = 230 cm.

180 cm (width of track) x 2.25 (heading fullness) = 405 cm. 405 cm divided by the width of fabric, i.e. 137 cm = 2.9 widths per window.

Note: This should be rounded up to a full width, i.e. 3 widths (1½ widths per curtain).

Multiply the number of widths by the finish drop of the curtain plus its turnings:

230 cm + 30 cm turnings (20 cm for the hem plus 10 cm for the heading) = 260 cm cut drop. See Headings on pages 89–95 for the appropriate heading allowance.

2.6 m x 3 widths = 7.8 metres of fabric required.

Imperial example:
Track length = 71 in. Finished drop = 91 in.

71 in (width of track) x 2.25 (heading fullness) = 160 in. 160 in divided by the width of fabric, i.e. 54 in = 2.9 widths per window.

Note: This should be rounded up to a full width, i.e. 3 widths (1½ widths per curtain).

Multiply the number of widths by the finish drop of the curtain plus its turnings:

91 in + 12 in turnings (8 in for the hem plus 4 in for the heading) = 103 in cut drop. See Headings on pages 89–95 for the appropriate heading allowance.

103 in x 3 widths = 309 in or 8.6 yards of fabric required.

CALCULATING PATTERNED FABRIC QUANTITIES

If you are using a patterned fabric, don't forget to take into account the fabric's pattern repeat:

Example: Pattern repeat = 68 cm (27 in)

Divide the finished cut drop by the pattern repeat:

260 cm (103 in) cut drop divided by a pattern repeat of 68 cm (27 in) = 3.8 pattern repeats. Round up to the next whole pattern repeat = 4 pattern repeats. Therefore, the fabric required for this patterned example is 4 x 68 cm (27 in)= 272 cm (108 in) instead of 260 cm (103 in) per cut drop.

Once armed with this information, you can purchase your fabric and linings and you are then ready to make your chosen curtains.

FABRIC QUANTITIES FOR HEADINGS

	Fullness	Pleat allowance
Commercial tapes	Follow manufacturer's recommendations	
Gathers	2–2.5 times	
Triple pleats	2.25–2.5 times	15–20 cm (6–8 in)
Double & champagne pleats	2–2.25 times	12–15 cm (4½–6 in)
Goblet pleats	2.25–2.5 times	12–18 cm (4½–7 in)
Box pleats	2.5–3 times	15–20 cm (6–8 in)
Cartridge pleats	2 times	6–8 cm (2¼–3¼ in)

MACHINE-MADE LINED CURTAINS

This is the quickest method of making a pair of curtains. As the stitching will be visible, you need to be neat and accurate with your machine stitching.

TO MAKE

1 Take the measurements of your windows and complete the measuring chart (see page 39). Calculate the fabric quantities required. See Estimating fabric quantities on pages 80–1.

2 Cut out the fabric lengths, taking into account any pattern repeats. The cut drop should include 20 cm (8 in) for the hem and allowances for the heading. See Headings on pages 89–95. Cut out the same amount of lining fabric. Join any widths of lining fabric together and press the seams flat.

3 Turn up a double 7 cm (2¾ in) hem and machine stitch in place, close to the folded edge. Press and put to one side.

4 Trim the selvedges of patterned fabric as required, leaving a 1.5 cm (⅝ in) seam allowance.

5 Join any fabric panels together and press the seams flat. See Pattern matching on pages 35–7.

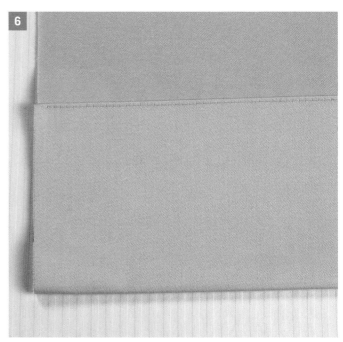

6 Turn up a double 10 cm (4 in) hem and machine stitch in place, close to the folded edge.

7 Trim the outside edges of the lining fabric so that it is 7.5 cm (3 in) narrower than the fabric.

8 Place the lining on the fabric, right sides together, positioned 3 cm (1¼ in) up from the bottom of the hem. The tops of the hems should be in line with each other. Machine stitch the sides together with a 1.5 cm (⅝ in) seam allowance.

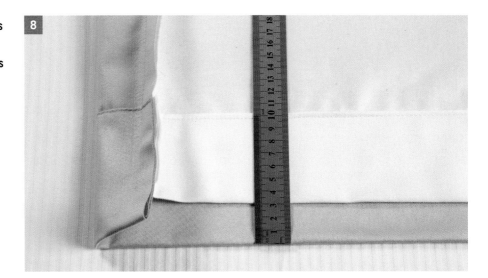

9 Turn the fabrics through to the right sides and press flat, with even amounts of turnings on each side. Quick mitre the corners at the hem, and slip stitch in place to neaten.

Note: This process is often referred to as 'bagging-in'.

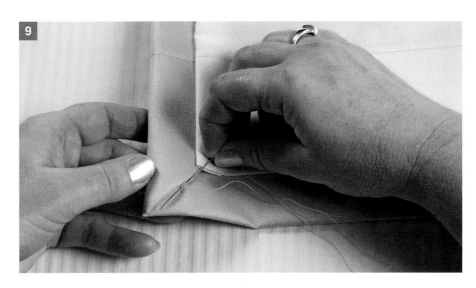

10 Measure up from the bottom edge and mark the curtain's finished drop point with pins. Transfer the pins to the right side of the fabric. You are now ready to work your chosen heading.

HAND-STITCHED UNLINED CURTAINS

This is the simplest of curtains to make and can be either machine-stitched or stitched by hand. I prefer my curtains to be hand-stitched as the hang and drape of hand-stitched curtains always look better. However, if you do decide to machine-stitch your curtains, make sure the machine stitch is neat and straight and positioned close to the folded edges.

TO MAKE

1 Take the measurements of your windows and complete the measuring chart (see page 39). Calculate the fabric quantities required. See Estimating fabric quantities on pages 80–1.

2 Cut out the fabric lengths, taking into account any pattern repeats. The cut drop should include 10 cm (4 in) for the hem and allowances for the heading. See Headings on pages 89–95.

3 Join any widths of fabric together, pattern-matching and pressing the seams as required. See Pattern matching on pages 35–7.

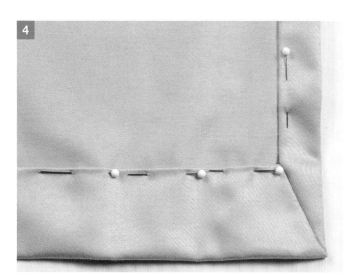

4 With rights sides of the fabric down, turn up a double 5 cm (2 in) hem and pin in place. Turn in a double 2.5 cm (1 in) side turning and pin in place. Mitre the corners using a long mitre so that the sides meet neatly. See Mitres on pages 46–7.

5 Stitch corner weights into the corners and at the base of any joins in the fabric. See Corner weights on page 45.

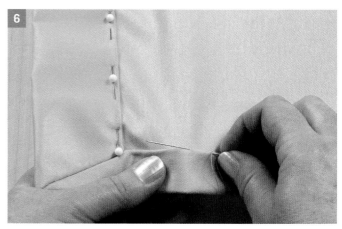

6 Slip stitch the side turnings, using a stitch length of 1.5 cm (⅝ in). Slip stitch the mitres, using a stitch length of 6 mm (¼ in).

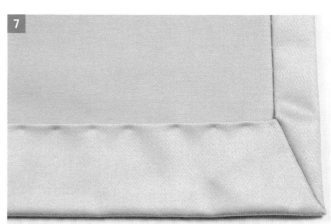

7 Stitch the hem in place using a hand stitched blind hem stitch. Alternatively, you can machine stitch close to the folded edge of the hem and side turnings.

8 Measure up from the bottom edge and mark the curtain's finished drop point with pins. Transfer the pins to the right side of the fabric. You are now ready to work your chosen heading.

HAND-STITCHED LINED CURTAINS

I find that when you hand-stitch curtains you have more control. Once linings are introduced, they will look tailored and more professional.

TO MAKE

1 Take the measurements of your windows and complete the measuring chart (see page 39). Calculate the fabric quantities required. See Estimating fabric quantities on pages 80–1.

2 Cut out the fabric lengths, taking into account any pattern repeats. The cut drop should include 20 cm (8 in) for the hem and allowances for the heading. See Headings on pages 89–95. Cut out the same amount of lining fabric. Join any widths of lining fabric together and press the seams flat.

3 Turn up a double 7 cm (2¾ in) hem on the lining and machine stitch in place, close to the folded edge. Press and put to one side.

4 Join any widths of main fabric together, pattern-matching and pressing the seams as required. See Pattern matching on pages 35–7.

5 With right sides of the fabric down, turn up a double 10 cm (4 in) hem and pin in place. Turn in 5 cm (2 in) side turnings and pin in place.

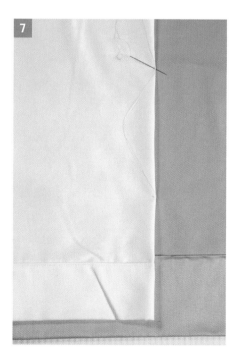

6 Mitre the corners using a true mitre and stitch corner weights into the corners and at the base of any joins. See Mitres (pages 46–7) and Corner weights (page 45). Serge stitch the side turnings, using a stitch length of 5 cm (2 in). The stitches should be barely visible on the front of the fabric. Slip stitch the mitres, using a stitch length of 6 mm (¼ in). Stitch the hem in place using a hand-stitched blind hem stitch.

7 Lay the lining fabric on top of the curtain fabric, wrong sides together. Position the hem 3 cm (1¼ in) up from the bottom edge of the curtain. The top of both hems should be in line with each other. Fold the lining fabric back and lock stitch the lining fabric to the curtain fabric every third of a width. Make sure you match the colour of the thread to the curtain fabric.

8 Reposition the lining and turn under the sides, 3 cm (1¼ in) from the outside edge, and pin in place. The corners of the lining should now be in line with the mitred corner of the curtain fabric.

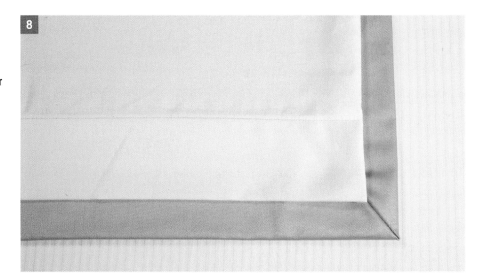

9 Slip stitch the lining fabric to the curtain fabric using a stitch length of 1.5 cm (⅝ in). Reduce the length of your stitch to 6 mm (¼ in) and slip stitch 10 cm (4 in) along the bottom edge of the lining, securing the ends firmly.

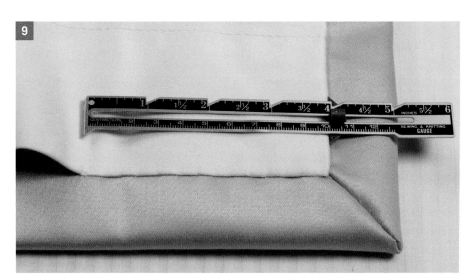

10 Make and fit a chain bar every half width and at the joins in fabric. See Chain bars on page 45.

11 Measure from the bottom edge and mark the curtain's finished drop point with pins. Transfer the pins to the right side of the fabric. You are now ready to work your chosen heading.

INTERLINED CURTAINS

For the best results, interlined curtains should be hand-stitched and any excess interlining cut off at the curtain's finished drop point to avoid bulk.

1 Take the measurements of your windows and complete the measuring chart (see page 39). Calculate the fabric quantities required. See Estimating fabric quantities on pages 80–1.

2 Cut out the fabric lengths, taking into account any pattern repeats. The cut drop should include 20 cm (8 in) for the hem and allowances for the heading. See Headings on pages 89–95.

3 Join any widths of fabric together, pattern-matching and pressing the seams as required. See Pattern matching on pages 35–7. Join any widths of lining together and press the seams flat. Turn up a double 7 cm (2¾ in) hem on the lining fabric and machine stitch in place close to the folded edge. Press and put to one side.

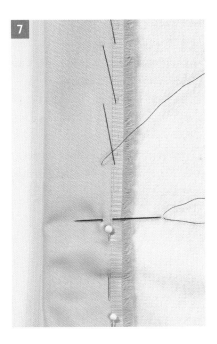

4 Join any widths of interlining together using a single lapped seam.

5 With the curtain fabric right side down, place the interlining on the wrong side of the fabric, 10 cm (4 in) up from the bottom edge of the fabric. Fold the interlining back and lock stitch in place every third of a width. The stitches should be barely visible on the front of the fabric.

6 Turn up a double 10 cm (4 in) hem enclosing the interlining and pin in place. Turn in the sides 5 cm (2 in) and pin in place. Mitre the corners and stitch corner weights in the corners and at the base of any joins.

7 Serge stitch the sides to the interlining using a stitch length of 5 cm (2 in). No stitches should be visible on the front of the fabric.

8 Slip stitch the mitred corners using a stitch length of 6 mm (¼ in).

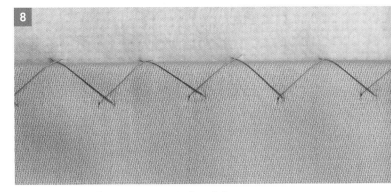

9 Herringbone stitch the hem to the interlining.

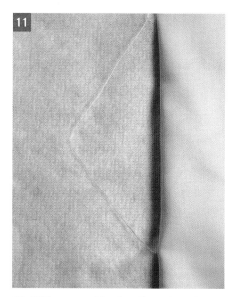

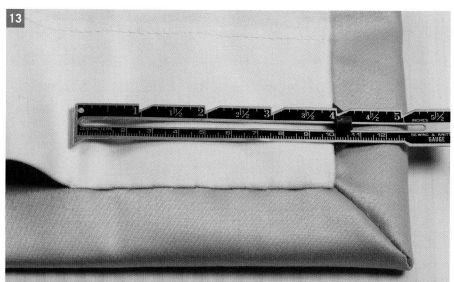

10 With wrong sides together, place the lining fabric 3 cm (1¼ in) up from the bottom edge of the hem. The tops of both hems should be in line with each other.

11 Fold the lining fabric back and lock stitch the lining to the interlining every third of a width.

12 Turn under the sides of the lining, 3 cm (1¼ in) from the edge of the fabric. The corner of the lining fabric should line up with the mitre.

13 Slip stitch the sides using a stitch length of 1.5 cm (⅝ in). Then reduce the stitch length to 6 mm (¼ in) and slip stitch 10 cm (4 in) in along the bottom edge of the lining.

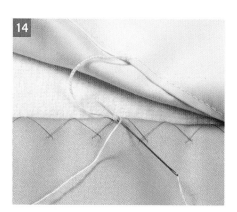

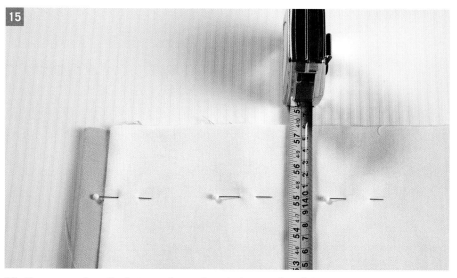

14 Make and fit chain bars at every seam and half width.

15 Measure up from the bottom edge and mark the curtain's finished drop point with pins. Cut off any excess interlining at this point and transfer the pins to the right side of the fabric. You are now ready to work your chosen heading.

HEADINGS

There is a large choice of headings to choose from. Some are very easy and simple to do, while others will need more time and patience to work out the correct spacing to finish them neatly.

When choosing your style of heading you will need to think about a few things:

- Will the curtains need to be drawn regularly, or are they just for show? Some of the headings may be difficult, if not impossible, to draw.
- What type of track/pole system is to be used?
- Will the heading be seen or will it be hidden behind a pelmet?
- Will the curtain be suspended below the track/pole or will the heading need to cover the track?
- Do you want the curtains to fall in neat, even folds?

- Are you prepared to keep 'dressing-in' your curtains?

The headings have been placed in order of complexity.

> **TIP** When using a commercial heading tape you can stitch the lining fabric right to the top of each side, but if you are making hand-stitched headings, you will need to leave the top 20 cm (8 in) free in order to insert the heading buckram.

NARROW HEADING TAPE WITH A TOP FRILL

Simple lined curtains with a small heading tape can look very effective with a small frill of approximately 2.5 cm (1 in) just above the tape. You will need an extra 5 cm (2 in) plus a seam allowance of 1.5 cm (⅝ in) to create a 2.5 cm (1 in) deep frill.

TO MAKE

1 Measure 6.5 cm (2½ in) from the finished drop point, and cut off any excess fabric as required.

2 Turn the top of the fabric down 4 cm (1½ in) (2.5 cm / 1 in for the frill + 1.5 cm / ⅝ in for the seam allowance) and pin in place.

3 Using a narrow heading tape, knot one end of the cords and turn under the raw edge.

4 Position the tape 2.5 cm (1 in) down from the top of the frill and, working from the leading edge of the curtain, pin in place. Leave the cords free at the back edge of the curtain but turn under the raw edge of the tape and pin in place. Make a cord pocket and insert under the tape at the back edge of the curtain, in line with the edge of the lining. Machine stitch along the top and bottom of the heading tape close to the outside edges.

5 Slip stitch the ends of the frill closed. Pull up the tape as required.

TIP When machining on heading tape, machine down one side and the bottom end. Then take the fabric out and machine across the top end and down the other side. You should never machine around the tape in one direction as this will create distortion.

PULLING UP CURTAIN TAPES

1 When pulling up the curtain fabric on the cords, pull the fabric to its tightest. Measure the cords to the required width of the curtain and tie a knot in the cords.

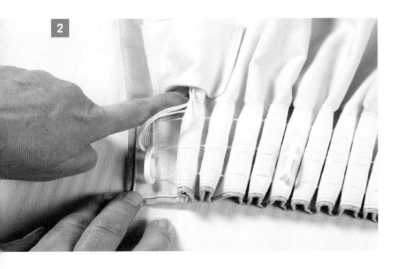

2 Even out the gathers along the cords. Twist the remaining cord and place in the cord pocket. Alternatively, you could use a commercial cord tidy. Place hooks, evenly spaced along the tape, approximately 10 cm (4 in) apart.

PENCIL PLEAT TAPE

This is the standard style of commercial heading tape. However, there is a wide range of styles and sizes, so make the appropriate allowances as required. For a 7.5 cm (3 in) heading tape you will need an extra 5 cm (2 in) for the heading turnings.

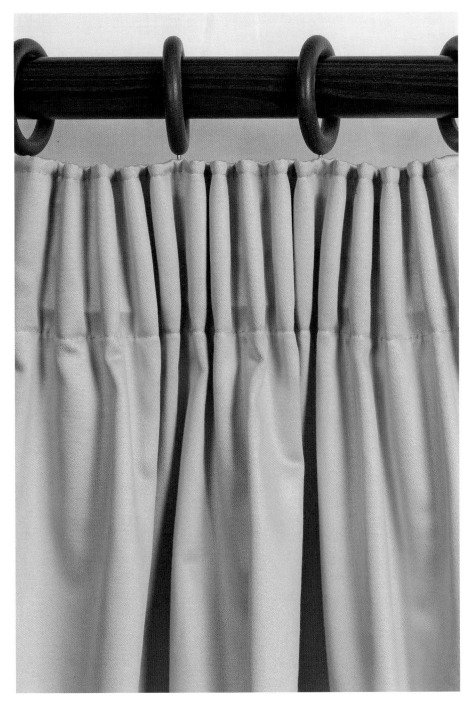

1 Measure 5 cm (2 in) from the curtain's finished drop point and cut off any excess fabric as required. Turn the top of the fabric down at the finished drop point.

2 Cover the raw edges with the pencil pleat tape, positioned 6 mm (¼ in) down from the top edge and pin in place.

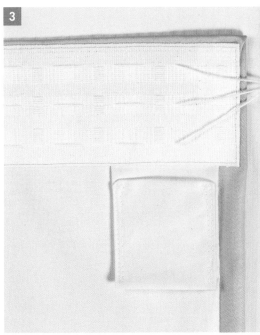

3 Insert a cord pocket under the bottom edge of the heading tape, in line with the lining.

4 Machine stitch the tape in place, stitching close to the edges of the tape. Pull up the cords as required.

PUFFED HEADING WITH TAPE

This puffed heading is created with excess fabric on or above heading tape. You will need between 15–20 cm (6–8 in) of extra fabric to create the puff, which can be stiffened with net to make the puff more effective. This is particularly useful on flimsy fabrics.

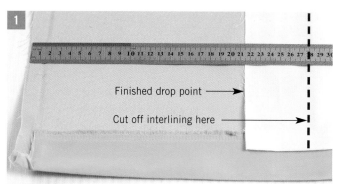

Finished drop point →

Cut off interlining here →

1 If you are using interlining, cut the excess off 6 cm (2¼ in) below the finished drop point. Use pins to hold the various layers together. Cut off the excess lining fabric at the finished drop point. From the finished drop point measure 20 cm (8 in) plus 1.5 cm (⅝ in) seam allowance and cut off any excess fabric.

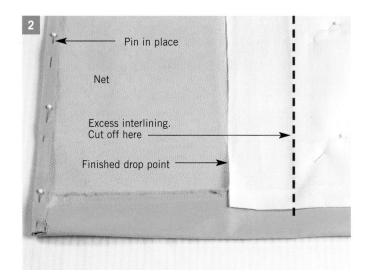

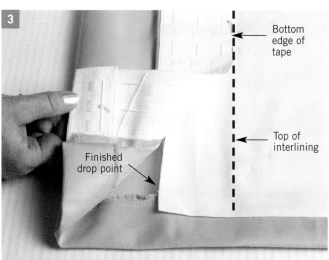

2 Cut a piece of netting 40 cm (16 in) deep by the width of the curtain. Fold the net in half and place on the wrong side of the fabric just above the finished drop point. Turn down the top edge of the fabric 1.5 cm (⅝ in), enclosing the top edge of the net, and pin in place.

3 Attach the heading tape to the top edge of the fabric. Turn the heading tape down, lining up the top edge of the tape with the finished drop point. Note that the bottom edge of the tape should enclose any interlining. Machine stitch the bottom edge of the tape in place.

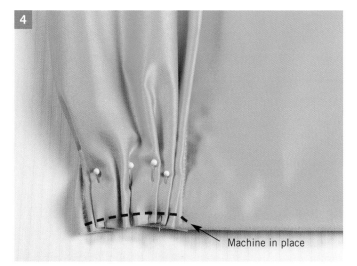

4 Turn the fabric to the right side and pleat the excess puff fabric at each end of the tape. Machine stitch in place.

5 Pull up the tape to the required width and tie off the cords. Arrange the puffed heading and stab stitch, at regular intervals along the length of the tape to hold the puffs in place.

ENCASED GATHERED HEADING

Encased headings are static headings where the fabric is ruched up on a pole. Light- or heavier-weight fabric can be used. This style of heading is ideal for café-style curtains, sheers and voiles. When joined together in the centre they need to be held back with ties or holdbacks.

When calculating the fabric required you will need to add enough fabric for a channel for the pole and for the frill above it.

• Measure the diameter of the pole and multiply by two for the depth of the channel: i.e. 2.5 cm (1 in) diameter x 2 = 5 cm (2 in).

• The depth of frill above the pole can be anything from 1.5 cm (⅝ in) on sheers to 7.5 cm (3 in) for heavyweight fabrics.

For a pole with a diameter of 2.5 cm (1 in) and a 6 cm (2½ in) frill depth.

1 Measure and mark 12 cm (5 in) from the finished drop point (2 x 6 cm / 2½ in) for the frill.

2 Measure and mark a further 10 cm (4 in) (2 x 5 cm / 2 in) for the pole's channel. Cut off any excess fabric as required.

3 Turn down the 12 cm (5 in) for the frill to meet at the finished drop point and pin in place.

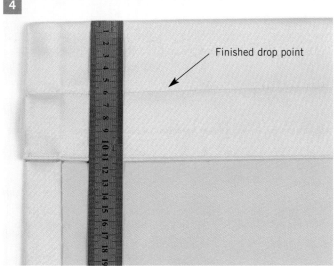

Finished drop point

4 Fold the remaining 10 cm (4 in) to form a double 5 cm (2 in) channel for the pole and pin in place. Machine stitch close to the bottom edge of the channel and at its top edge. You should now have a 5 cm (2 in) deep channel with a 6 cm (2¼ in) frill above it.

5 Slip stitch the ends of the frill closed. Insert the pole and ruche the fabric evenly.

HAND-STITCHED HEADINGS

A hand-stitched heading will always look tailored and more professional. There is a wide range of hand-stitched headings for you to choose from, and to make them look their best, care must be taken when calculating the pleat and space allowances.

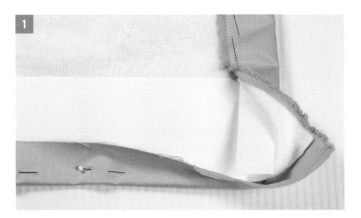

FINISHING FOR HAND-STITCHED HEADINGS

1 With the wrong side of the fabric up, insert the heading buckram along the top edge of the curtain, in line with its finished drop point, and pin in place. Excess interlining should also be cut off at this point. To support the leading and back edges of the curtain, give yourself a 2.5 cm (1 in) turning at each end of the heading buckram. Fold the top fabric down over the heading buckram, cutting off any excess fabric that may show below the buckram, and pin in place.

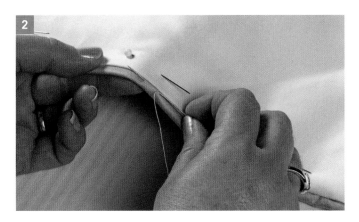

2 Turn under the lining fabric, cutting off any excess fabric as required, and pin in place. Slip stitch the lining 6 mm (¼ in) from the top edge of the fabric, using a 1.5cm (⅝ in) stitch length.

Note: Keep any holding pins in place until you have marked the position of the heading pleats.

Now you are ready to work your chosen pleat formation. See Pleat calculations (page 96) and Pleat formations (pages 98–103).

HOOK POSITION

Hooks are positioned in the back of the pleats. The top of the pin's suspension point should be positioned 1.5 cm (⅝ in) down from the top of the curtain. This positioning will give the curtain a 1.5 cm (⅝ in) clearance above the floor or sill.

PLEAT CALCULATIONS

Regardless of what type of hand-stitched heading you want to do, you must first calculate the number and size of the pleats.

First make a note of a few measurements:
- Width of the track or pole, i.e. 180 cm (71 in)
- Length of the curtain's leading edge/overlap
- Length of the curtain's return
- Finished fabric width of each curtain, i.e. 2 widths = 261 cm (103 in)
- Number of widths of fabric used, i.e. 4 widths
- Tolerance (amount of fabric needed to allow for spring-back)

Note: On average you will get four pleats or goblets to a width of fabric, more for cartridge pleats.

Example:

```
  180 cm  (71 in) = length of track/pole
+ 15 cm  (6 in) = 2 x 7.5 cm (3 in) leading edges/overlap
+ 15 cm  (6 in) = 2 x 7.5 cm (3 in) returns
+ 12 cm  (5 in) = tolerance for spring-back (3 cm/1¼ in
                     per width of fabric)
```
_____

222 cm (88 in) divided by 2 = 111 cm (44 in) (finished width of each curtain)

Therefore:

261 cm (103 in) = finished fabric width
- 111 cm (44 in) = leading edge, return and space allowances
_____

150 cm (59 in) = pleats allowance

Now:

111 cm (44 in) less 7.5 cm (3 in) leading edge and 7.5 cm (3 in) return = 96 cm (38 in) space allowance

Divide 96 cm (38 in) (space allowance) by 7 spaces = 13.7 cm (5½ in)
Divide 150 cm (59 in) by 8 pleats = 18.75 cm (7⅜ in)

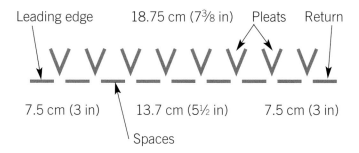

Leading edge   18.75 cm (7⅜ in)   Pleats   Return

7.5 cm (3 in)   13.7 cm (5½ in)   7.5 cm (3 in)

Spaces

Note: If the pleat size is too small (less than 15 cm/6 in), or too big (more than 20 cm/8 in), decrease or increase the number of pleats accordingly.

PLEATING PATTERNED FABRICS

If you want to arrange the pleats and spaces around the pattern or stripe on the fabric, you will need to work the calculations slightly differently. To be sure that you have the correct spacings and fabric quantities, I suggest that you work the pleats and spacings across the top of the fabric before fully making the curtain.

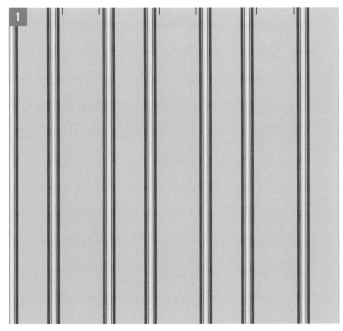

1 In order to calculate the size of the pleats, place pins either side of the pattern or stripe that you wish to be centred within each pleat.

2 Work across the width of the fabric to determine the number of pleats.

3 To calculate the size of the spaces, deduct the leading edge, return and tolerance measurements from the finished fabric width. Divide this number by the number of spaces between each pleat.

4 If there is not enough fabric to allow for the leading edge, return and tolerance plus the turnings, then you will need to reduce the number of pleats by one. Cut off any excess fabric over and above the turning allowances.

PLEAT FORMATIONS

This section describes the formation of the various heading pleats that you can create.

1 For most hand-stitched headings you will need 10 cm (4 in) for turnings. Calculate the pleats and spacings and mark with pins along the top of the curtain. See Pleat calculations on page 96.

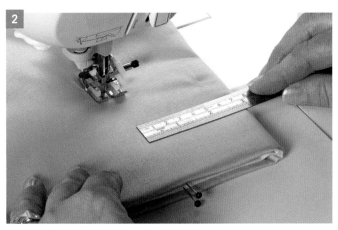

2 Fold and hold the pleats in place with pins. Place the curtain under the sewing machine's presser foot and machine stitch the back of the pleats in place. Now form your chosen pleat.

TIP When machining in pleats, I work from the bottom of the pleat to the top. This way I can support and lay the fabric out before me. Use a small ruler to measure half the width of the pleat. Stitch from the bottom of the heading buckram to the top, doing a reverse stitch at each end to secure the threads.

TRIPLE PLEATS

Triple pleats should be between 15–20 cm (6–8 in) wide.

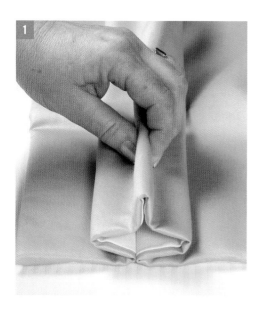

1 Grasping the centre of the pleat, push down on the pleat to form three equal parts.

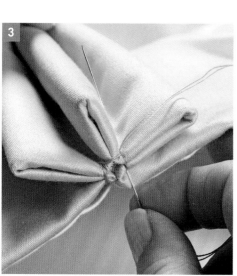

2 Neatly over-sew the bottom edge of the pleats to hold the pleat in place.

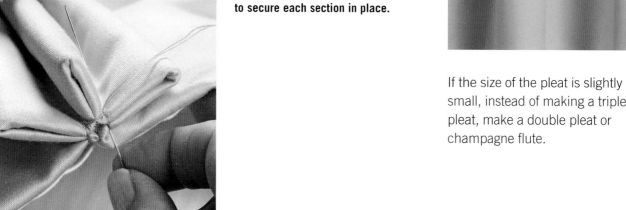

3 Over-sew the top of the pleat to secure each section in place.

DOUBLE PLEATS

If the size of the pleat is slightly small, instead of making a triple pleat, make a double pleat or champagne flute.

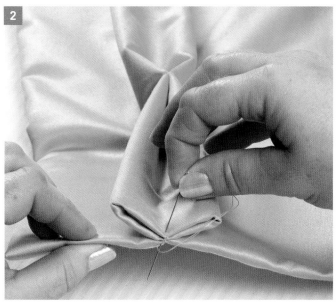

1 Push the pleat flat and then bring the bottom outside edges together in the centre and neatly over-sew to keep in place.

2 Over-sew in the centre at the top of the pleat to help keep its shape.

CHAMPAGNE FLUTE

A champagne flute is a small version of a goblet pleat.

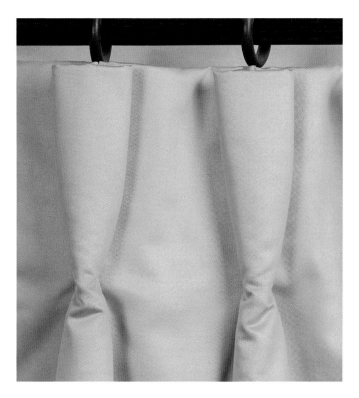

1 Push the pleat flat and then nip the bottom outside edges together at the back of the pleat. Stab stitch through the back of the pleat to hold in place. Leave the top edge free.

GOBLET PLEATS

Goblet pleats are best suited to static headings as they are quite bulky to stack-back.

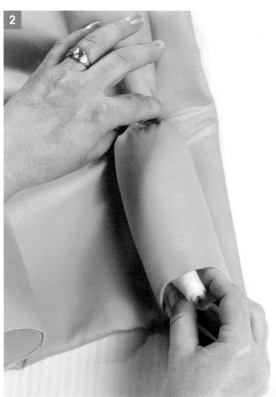

2 Shape the pleat into a nice goblet shape and stuff with off-cuts of rolled up interlining.

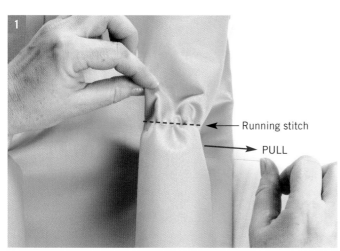

1 Using a strong thread, place a small running stitch around the base of the pleat. Pull tight and secure the ends at the back of the pleat.

Note: If the top of the goblet can be seen (on a staircase for instance), cover a circle of heading buckram, the diameter of the goblet, with fabric and, using a curved needle, slip stitch in place over the stuffing.

BOX PLEATS

Box pleats are best suited to static headings. Spaced box pleats do not stack-back well and touching box pleats will not stack-back at all.

INVERTED PLEATS

Inverted pleats are small, reversed cartridge pleats formed at the back of the curtain. They can be formed by either leaving the fold free at the back, which allows for easier stack-back, or they can be formed as reverse box pleats, which lie flat against the back of the heading, but this allows limited stack-back.

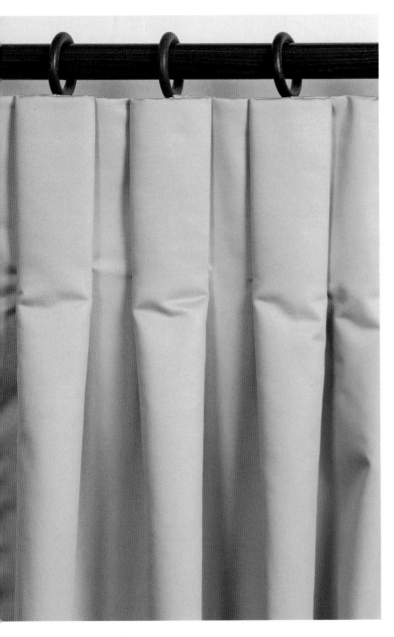

Push the pleat flat and over-sew the outside edges at the top and bottom of the pleat. Make sure the bottom stitches are made on the back edge of the pleat so as not to be seen.

CARTRIDGE PLEATS

Cartridge pleats are large, spaced pencil pleats. They are very simple to form and are ideal for fine fabrics, but because of the small amount of fabric held within the pleat, you should be aware that they will not hold the fold of the pleat right to the hem of the curtain as with other types of pleats, causing the fabric to A-line out at the bottom. This is a particular problem if you are using interlining.

Cartridge pleats are between 6–8 cm (2¼–3¼ in) wide and you will need two times the fabric's fullness. Because of their smallness, calculating the pleats and spacings is slightly different.

Measure the finished width of the curtain.

Deduct the amount of the leading edge and the return, and divide the remaining fabric by the width of the cartridge pleat required.

261 cm (103 in) = finished width of curtain
- 15 cm (6 in) (7.5 cm/3 in leading edge + 7.5 cm/3 in return)
––––––––––
246 cm (97 in) divided by 7 cm (2¾ in) wide pleats = 35

(18 pleats and 17 spaces of 7 cm/2¾ in) each with a leading edge and return of 7.5 cm/3 in each)

Note: Always try to end with an odd number or you will need to recalculate the spacings accordingly.

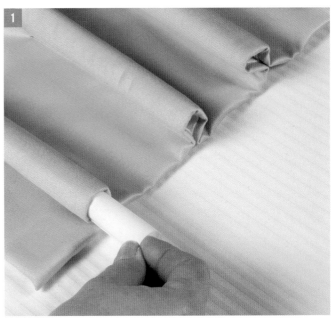

1 Position the pleats and the spacings along the top edge of the curtain with pins. Pin the pleats together with a holding pin. Machine stitch the back of the pleats. Stuff the cartridge pleats with off-cuts of rolled up heading buckram.

TAB TOP CURTAINS

Tab top curtains are usually lined but not normally interlined. They are best as a static heading as they do not draw easily, and if drawn back, the tab top effect will be lost.

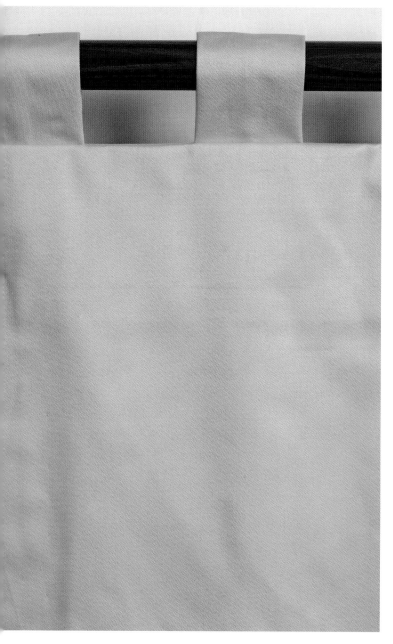

You will need one and a half times the fullness to make these curtains.

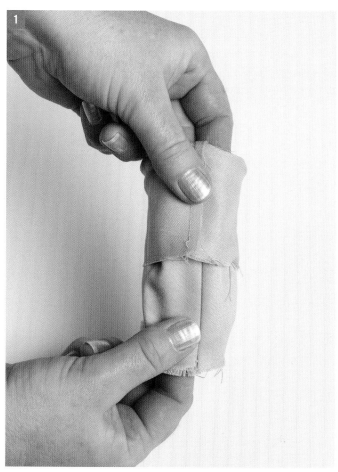

1 **Make the curtains in the usual way, with a 1.5 cm (⅝ in) top seam allowance. Cut out the tab fabric: 15 cm (6 in) wide x 25 cm (10 in) deep. Fold the tab fabric in half lengthways and machine stitch down the side with a 1 cm (⅜ in) seam allowance. Turn the fabric through and press flat with the seam positioned at the centre back.**

2

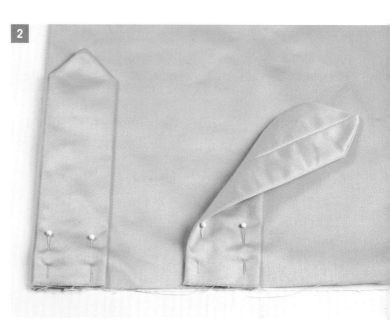

2

2 Fold the tabs in half and, with raw edges together, position them evenly along the top of the curtain. Pin in place with raw edges together. For most poles you will need fabric tabs with a depth of at least 7.5 cm (3 in), but for larger poles you may need to increase the tab's depth. Don't forget to deduct the tab's depth from the finished drop point when making the body of the curtain.

3 Cut a piece of fabric for the facing, 15 cm (6 in) deep by the width of the curtain fabric. Iron a fusible interlining or buckram to the back of the facing.

4 With raw edges together, place the facing over the tabs and machine stitch in place, with a 1.5 cm (⅝ in) seam allowance. Turn the facing to the back of the curtain. Fold the raw edges under and slip stitch to the lining fabric.

Alternatively, for a more decorative tab top finish:

2 Turn the fabric through to the right side and press flat. Make the curtains in the usual way, with a 1.5 cm (⅝ in) top seam allowance. With raw edges together, position the tabs evenly along the top of the curtain and pin in place. Continue to make the curtain in the usual way (see Steps 3 and 4 of basic tabs)

1

1 Fold the tab fabric in half lengthways and machine stitch down the side. Position the seam at the centre back and machine stitch one end of the tab to a point.

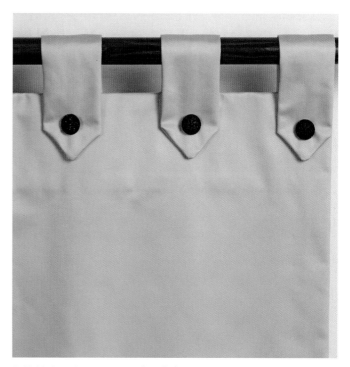

3 Fold the tabs over and stitch in place making sure the tabs are all the same length. Use a button or other decorative device to finish.

EYELET CURTAINS

The fabric fullness required for eyelet curtains is between 1.5 and 2 times the width of the pole/track. Often, it is better to use the eyelet tape to determine the width required, and then to make the curtain to that width. Don't forget to allow for spring-back.

USING EYELET TAPE WITH NO VISIBLE STITCHING

You will need an even number of eyelets along the top of the curtain. They are evenly spaced and are positioned at least 5 cm (2 in) in from each end and 4 cm (1½ in) down from the top edge of the curtain.

When measuring the finished drop of the curtain, measure from the top of the pole to the finished drop and add 4 cm (1½ in) to this measurement for the allowance above the eyelets, plus 10 cm (4 in) for turnings.

1 **Make the curtains in the usual way. With wrong side of the fabric up, measure and mark the finished drop point of the curtain with pins. Cut off any excess interlining 4 cm (1½ in) above this point. Leave the pins in place so that the interlining does not move.**

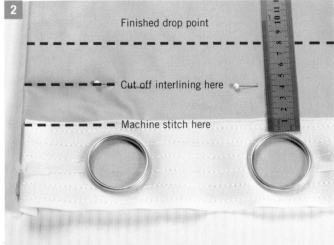

Finished drop point

Cut off interlining here

Machine stitch here

2 **Position the tape so that the top of the eyelets are 8 cm (3 in) from the finished drop point. Machine stitch the tape in place along the top edge only.**

3 Turn the top edge fabric and tape down in line with the finished drop point, taking out any holding pins. Quick mitre the ends of the tape and pin in place.

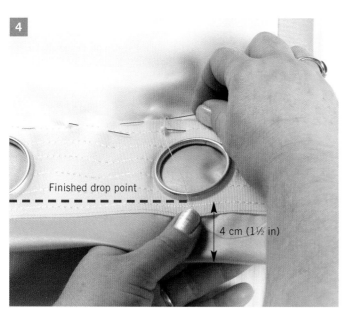

Finished drop point

4 cm (1½ in)

4 Cut off any excess lining and slip stitch the bottom edge of the tape to the lining. Slip stitch the ends closed.

5 Pin around each eyelet to hold the layers firmly together.

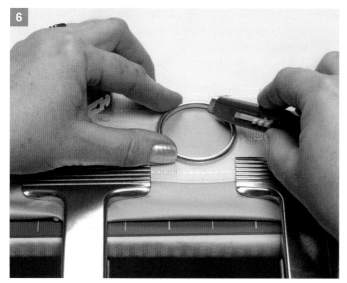

6 Cut out the eyelets using a scalpel, making sure to use a cutting board. Use clamps to hold the fabric securely in place. Firm pressure is required. Try a sample first to iron out any snags, following all necessary Health and Safety procedures.

7 Attach the front of the eyelets and press firmly in place.

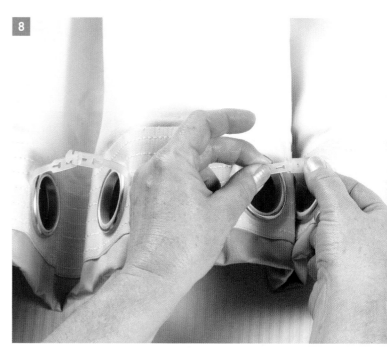

8 Connect the plastic spacers together, hang and dress the curtain.

Using an eyelet machine

1) Make the curtain in the normal manner but use fusible heading buckram ironed onto the top of the interlining. If you don't use fusible heading buckram, tack the heading buckram firmly in place so it does not move.

2) Finish the lining in the normal manner.

3) Evenly space and mark the position of the eyelets, i.e. 5 cm (2 in) in from each end, 8 cm (3¼ in) apart and 4 cm (1½ in) down. Using an eyelet machine cut the holes and attach the eyelets.

TIP If you don't have an eyelet machine and are using the loose snap-on eyelets, make sure the fabric is pinned and clamped firmly in place so that the fabrics do not move when cutting and fixing the eyelets.

SHEER CURTAINS

Sheer curtains need neat, even edges and a leaded tape running through the hem to weigh down the lightweight fabrics.

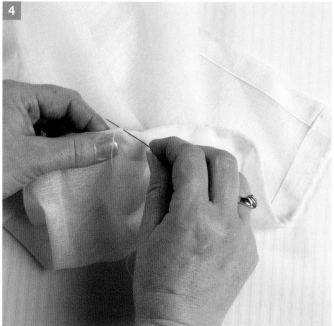

TO MAKE

- For sheers on a small brass rod with a diameter of 1.5 cm (⅝ in), the channel depth would be 3 cm (1¼ in).
- Add an amount for the frill above, i.e. 1.5 cm (⅝ in) making a depth of 4.5 cm (1¾ in).
- Multiply by two, for neat, even turnings, making 9 cm (3½ in) the total amount of extra fabric required for this heading.

1 When cutting out sheer fabrics, extra care must be taken to get even, straight edges. If at all possible, pull a thread to get a straight line.

2 Turn the sides in a double 1.5 cm (⅝ in), pin and machine in place close to the folded edge.

3 Turn the hem up a double 2 cm (¾ in) and machine in place. Using a safety pin, thread the lead weight through the hem.

4 Slip stitch the lead weight tape to the bottom of the hem using very small stitches so that the lead weight does not move about within the hem.

5 Measure 9 cm (3½ in) from the finished drop point and cut off any excess fabric as required. Turn the top of the fabric down at the finished drop point and form a double 4.5 cm (1¾ in) fold. Pin in place. Machine stitch close to the bottom of the folded edge.

6 Measure up from this point the depth of the channel, i.e. 3 cm (1¼ in), and place another row of machine stitches. Insert the rod and ruche the fabric evenly.

Alternatively, attach a transparent commercial heading tape or hand-stitch pleats using a transparent heading buckram.

TIE-BACKS

Tie-backs were traditionally made with starched-hessian buckram covered with bump interlining, but today we also use pelmet/tie-back buckrams.

Consider the overall effect tie-backs will make to your window display, as both style and position will have a bearing on proportion and balance. Place the tie-back hook on the wall in line with the outside edge of the curtain, as the vertical drape will be distorted if the hook is incorrectly positioned.

The height of the tieback hook is discretionary, but a height of approximately 1 m (3 ft 3 in) from the floor is generally a good height for most windows. For windows over 3 m (9 ft 8 in) high, the hook should be placed slightly higher. Don't fit the hook until the curtains have been hung, so that any adjustments can easily be made.

Measure the embrace of the curtains by holding a tape measure around the curtain.

Decide on the shape and style of tie-back to be used:

• Plain
• Banana
• Scalloped
• Plaited
• Ruched
• Rope or tassel

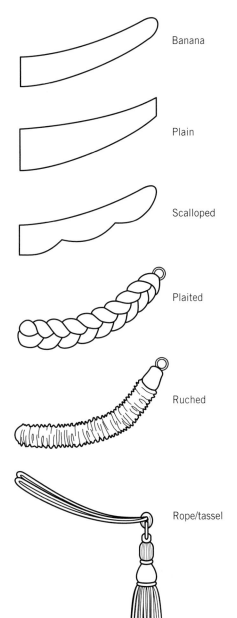

Banana

Plain

Scalloped

Plaited

Ruched

Rope/tassel

MAKING A PAPER PATTERN

If you are going to make a plain, banana or scalloped tie-back, you will need to make a paper pattern of the shape and size required.

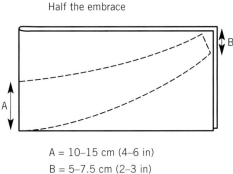

Half the embrace

A = 10–15 cm (4–6 in)
B = 5–7.5 cm (2–3 in)

PIPED TIE-BACKS

Piped tie-backs are the basic tie-backs used. They can be plain or shaped, but the process of making them is the same.

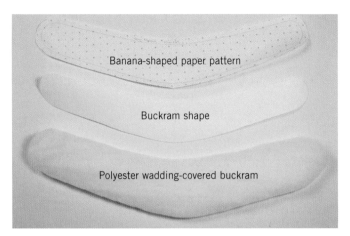

1 Make a paper pattern of the shape required: plain, banana or scalloped. Cut out the shape in buckram or pelmet/tie-back stiffening covered with wadding or interlining as required.

2 Cut out the fabric and lining fabric with a 1.5 cm ($^5/_8$ in) seam allowance all round. Remember to place any pattern on the front of the tie-back and don't forget you have a left and a right tie-back.

3 Make up the piping as required, and with raw edges together, stitch the piping on the right side of the fabric. Snip into the piping to ease it around the curves. Join the two ends of the piping. See Joining piping on page 53.

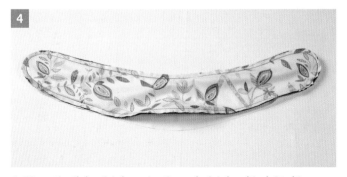

4 Place the lining fabric under the main fabric with right sides together, and machine stitch around the piping again. Leave a gap at the bottom edge large enough to insert the stiffening.

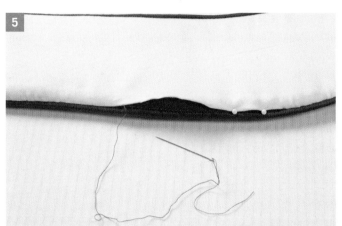

5 Snip and notch around the curves and turn the tie-back through to the right side. Press as necessary and insert the stiffening. Turn the seam allowance under and Slip stitch the bottom edge closed.

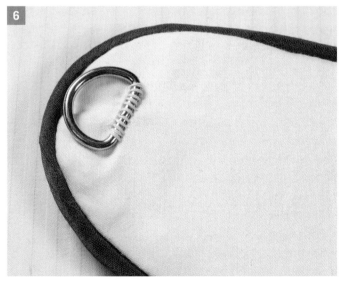

6 Attach brass rings at both ends, using a buttonhole stitch.

So that the rings are not visible, the front ring should be placed level with the edge of the tie-back and the back ring should be placed half over the edge to allow it to catch the tie-back hook neatly.

PLAITED TIE-BACKS

Plaited tie-backs, using both your main and contrast fabrics, is another effective way of creating tie-backs for your curtains.

1 Cut three strips of fabric 13 cm (5 in) deep by one width. Cut three strips of polyester wadding the same width and depth.

2 Fold the fabric in half with right sides together and machine stitch down the long edge with a 1 cm (⅜ in) seam allowance, forming a tube. Fold the polyester in half and machine stitch to one end of the fabric tube.

3 With the aid of a long ruler, turn the fabric through to the right side enclosing the polyester inside the tube. Repeat Steps 1 to 3 for all three strips of fabric.

4 Fix the three strips together at one end with a couple of holding stitches. Plait the strips together, stitching the other ends together when finished.

5 Cut two pieces of fabric 12 cm (5 in) wide by 7.5 cm (3 in) deep. Fold each piece in half and machine down the short edge with a 1 cm (⅜ in) seam allowance, forming a small tube 6 x 7.5 cm (2¼ x 3 in). Place the seam in the centre back of the strip of fabric and machine stitch across one end with a 1 cm (⅜ in) seam allowance.

6 Turn through to the right side forming a small end cap 5 cm (2 in) wide by 6.5 cm (2½ in) long. Trim back the wadding at each end of the plait. Place the end cap over the end of the plaited strips and turning the raw edges under, slip stitch in place. Do the same at the other end. Slip stitch a piece of cotton tape the length of the plait, to the back of the plait to hold the three strips firmly in place.

7 Attach brass rings at both ends, using a buttonhole stitch.

So that the rings are not visible, the front ring, A, should be placed level with the edge of the tie-back and the back ring, B, should be placed half over the edge to allow it to catch the tie-back hook.

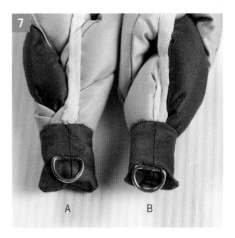

RUCHED TIE-BACKS

Another decorative tie-back is the ruched tie-back. This can be made in the same or a contract fabric. You will need twice the embrace measurement to create this ruched effect.

1 Roll a piece of polyester wadding, the length of the embrace, to 4 cm (1½ in) in diameter, and using a herringbone stitch, stitch in place.

2 Cut a piece of fabric 15 cm (6 in) deep by 2.5 times the embrace. Fold the fabric in half and stitch down the long edge to form a tube. Turn the fabric through to the right side.

3 Stitch a length of cotton tape to one end of the polyester roll, and using a large safety pin, pull the roll of polyester into the fabric tube. When the fabric reaches the end, secure the fabric to the polyester roll. Turn under the raw edges of the fabric and, inserting a brass ring, slip stitch the end closed.

4 Ruche all the excess fabric over the polyester roll, securing it at the other end. Slip stitch the end closed as before. Even out the fullness and stab stitch at intervals along the roll to hold the fabric in place.

VALANCES AND SKIRTS

Valances and skirts can be used on window treatments, bed valances and loose covers for chairs. They can be tailored, gathered or pleated, either with or without a yoke.

A window valance should be ⅕ to ⅙ of the length of the curtains. The yoke should be ⅓ of the depth of the finished valance, with the skirt ⅔ the finished depth.

On bedding and loose covers, the skirt can be full length or fitted to a yoke. The finished length of the skirt should be 1.5 cm (⅝ in) above the floor. See Bed valance on pages 136–37 and Loose cover on pages 150–55.

YOKED VALANCE WITH SPACED BOX PLEATS

A yoke on a valance is the flat piece of fabric that a pleated, gathered or shaped skirt is attached. The yoke can be stiffened with a piece of heading or pelmet buckram softened with a piece of wadding. Yokes also look good with piping defining the top and bottom edges.

To make a box pleated skirt you will need at least three times the width of the finished yoke, plus turning and seam allowances. I always allow extra to give me room to manoeuvre.

TIP When trying to calculate pleat sizes and spacing, cut a width of fabric 20 cm (8 in) deep to experiment with. Once you have decided on the pleat formation you can then accurately calculate the actual fabric requirements.

TO MAKE THIS EXAMPLE

1 Cut out the contrast fabric for the bottom edge of the skirt: 5 cm (2 in) deep plus 3 cm (1¼ in) seam allowances by the width required.

2 Cut out the main skirt and lining fabrics: the depth of the skirt plus 3 cm (1¼ in) seam allowances, less the 2.5 cm (1 in) depth of the contrast fabric.

3 With right sides together, stitch the contrast fabric to the bottom of the skirt fabric and the lining to the other side of the contrast fabric.

4 With right sides together, fold the skirt fabric so that there are equal amounts of contrast fabric, front and back. Machine close the ends and turn through to the right side. Alternatively, turn in the ends and slip stitch the lining to the main fabric. Press in place.

5 Mark every 5 cm (2 in) apart along the top edge of the skirt. Place the first mark at the back of the third mark and pin in place. Place the fifth mark at the back of the third mark and pin in place. Place the ninth mark at the back of the eleventh mark and pin in place. Place the thirteenth mark at the back of the eleventh mark and pin in place. Continue in this way for the length of the skirt.

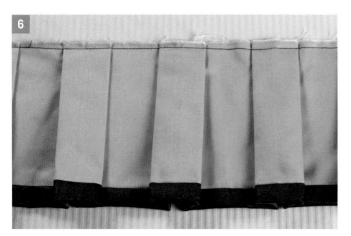

6 Machine a holding stitch along the top edge and press the pleats in place.

7 Cut out the yoke fabric, measuring the finished width and depth of the yoke, plus 1.5 cm (⅝ in) seam allowance all round.

8 Apply the appliqué detail to the yoke, working from the centre out. Satin stitch the edges of the appliqué design. See Appliqué on page 62.

9 Make up enough piping and attach to the top and bottom edges of the yoke.

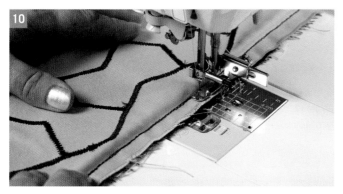

10 With right sides together, attach the pleated skirt to the bottom of the yoke and machine stitch in place.

11 Attach Velcro 2 cm (¾ in) down from the top edge of the yoke's lining fabric. With right sides together, machine stitch the yoke lining to the top of the yoke.

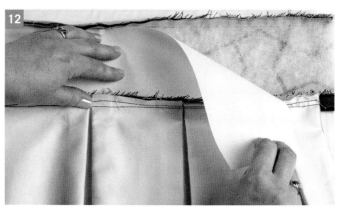

12 Cut a piece of buckram and wadding the size of the finished yoke and insert between the piped edges. Turn all the raw edges in towards the centre of the yoke.

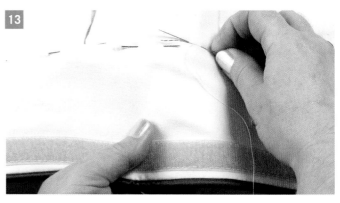

13 Fold the yoke lining down to cover the back of the yoke. Turn the raw edges under and slip stitch all around to neaten.

TOUCHING BOX PLEATS

1 Mark every 5 cm (2 in) apart along the top edge of the skirt fabric.

2 Place the first mark at the back of the second mark and pin in place. Place the fourth mark at the back of the second mark and pin in place. Place the sixth mark at the back of the eighth mark and pin in place. Place the tenth mark at the back of the eighth mark and pin in place. Continue in this way for the length of the skirt.

3 Machine stitch 1 cm (⅜ in) from the top edge of the skirt to hold the pleats in place.

PELMETS

Traditionally, like tie-backs, pelmets and lambrequins were made with starched-hessian buckram covered with bump interlining. Today, we still use buckram or sail cloth for traditional pelmets, as well as felted pelmet and tie-back buckram, but the current vogue for firm pelmets with clean lines means we can also use a range of modern firm materials such as plywood, medium density fibreboard and other composite boards, covered with a wadding of some kind: 6 mm (¼ in) foam, polyester wadding, interlinings or felted insulation pad.

Pelmets can be made with decorative panels inserted into the fabric, pleats, and appliqué applied to the fabric or various types of trimmings attached: piping, braids, gimp, fringes, tassels, etc.

Here I am going to show you how to make a firm pelmet using 6 mm (¼ in) plywood, covered with insulation pad to give a firm but padded effect. The pelmet will be fitted to the front edge and return of a pelmet board using Velcro.

First, you must decide on the shape of your pelmet:
- The depth of the pelmet should be ⅕ to ⅙ the length of the curtains, with the shallowest part of the pelmet covering the top of the window frame.
- Pelmets can be plain with straight lines, curved or combinations of both straight lines and curves; the variations are endless.
- Be aware that sharp, inverted angles on firm pelmets can be very hard to achieve, as it is difficult to get the fabric to turn in two directions without having to cut so close to the edge that the fabric is likely to fray.
- If you choose to create a pelmet with sharp angles, it would be better to fit a facing to the shape of the bottom edge. See Shaped edges on page 68.
- Cover the pelmet board with lining fabric and fix the hook side of Velcro to the front and return edges.

TO MAKE

1 Take the measurements of the pelmet board: front edge and return. The pelmet should be 1 cm (⅜ in) longer than the pelmet board.

2 Decide on the shape and design of the pelmet. Make a paper pattern of one half of the shape. Working from the centre of the pelmet, draw the shape. You can then mirror image the shape on the other side to make sure it is symmetrical.

3 Cut out the fabric, 10 cm (4 in) larger all round. Seam together and press flat any joins required. See Joining fabrics on page 37.

Note: If you want decorative panels applied or inserted into the fabric, now is the time to create them and to make any piping that may be required.

> **TIP** If you are using fabrics of different weights, it is better to top stitch the lighter fabric to the heavier fabric.

4 Draw the shape onto the plywood and cut out with a jigsaw. Be sure to take all relevant health and safety precautions. Cut two return pieces: the depth of the pelmet required by the depth of the pelmet board.

5 Place the front of the pelmet and the returns together with a 1 cm (⅜ in) gap between them.

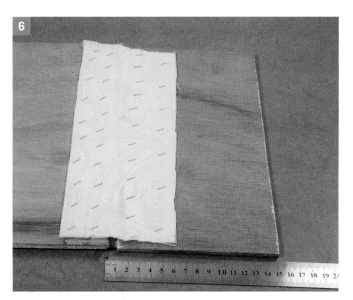

6 Using a spray adhesive, fabric glue or staples fix fabric hinges: 10 cm (4 in) wide by the depth of the pelmet, to both sides of the boards.

7 Cut a piece of insulation pad or wadding, 10 cm (4 in) larger than the pelmet. Cover the front of the pelmet board and staple off on the back edge. Keep the hinges pulled out taut and make neat square corners, cutting away any excess as required.

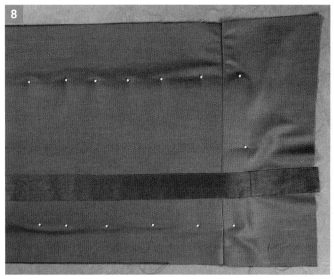

11 Staple the tabs on the top edge towards the back of each return. For very long pelmets, you may need a long tab in the centre of the pelmet to support the weight. Apply any trim or piping and staple to the bottom edge.

12 Cover the back of the pelmet with a piece of polyester wadding to even out the layers.

Return

8 Place the fabric on the pelmet; making sure it is centred properly. Working from the centre, smooth out and pin firmly in place.

9 Turn the pelmet over and staple the fabric off on the back. Make neat square corners and cut off any excess fabric.

10 Make two tabs 7.5 cm (3 in) wide x 7.5 cm (3 in) deep. Stitch the soft side of the Velcro to the top edge of each tab.

13 Cut a piece of lining fabric the finished width by the depth, plus 1.5 cm (⅝ in) seam allowance all round. Sew Velcro 2 cm (¾ in) down from the top edge of the lining.

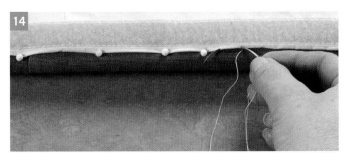

14 With the Velcro positioned 6 mm (¼ in) down from the top of the pelmet, and working from the centre out, pin the lining to the back. Turn the raw edges under, and using a curved needle, slip stitch the lining in place to neaten.

Note: If you are using piping, slip stitch through the piping with each stitch to hold the piping firmly in place and to stop it from rolling back.

TIP You can staple the lining to the back of the pelmet and then cover the staples with a gimp or braid. This can be very effective, particularly if the pelmet can be seen from both sides, for example at patio doors.

PELMET SHAPES

Pelmets can be made in various shapes. The following are just a few examples:

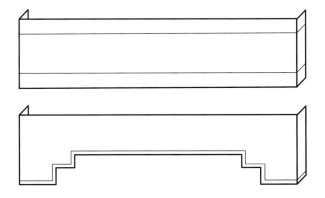

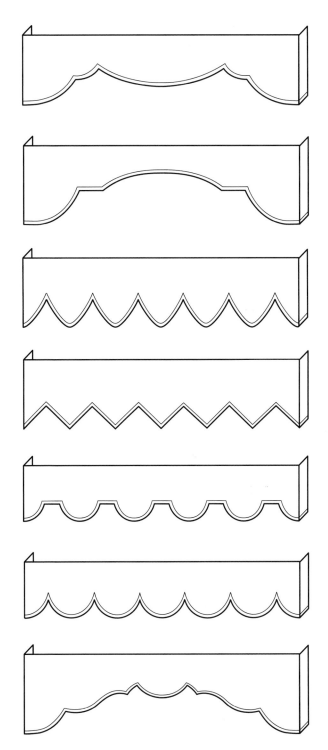

FASCIAS

Fascias are mini pelmets that are just the depth of the track system to be covered. They are padded with interlining and are made in the same way as firm pelmets.

CUSHIONS

There are three basic cushion constructions: scatter, box and bolster, and all other cushions are a variation of these in either shape or size.

CUSHION PADS

- Foam wrapped in stockinet – a very basic cushion with a flat appearance.
- Foam with a polyester wrap in stockinet – gives the foam a softer, more sumptuous appearance.
- Foam cores with a fibre fill wrap – stability from the foam but will need plumping to keep the effect.
- Foam with a feather wrap – stability from the foam but will still need plumping
- Fibre only – okay for back cushions but not recommended for seat cushions. Unless it is plumped regularly, it will flatten and go lumpy.
- Comforel by Dupont (fibre balls) – sumptuous but still needs plumping regularly.
- Feather – comes in various qualities from poultry to various mixes of duck and down. Will need regular plumping.
- Down feathers – the softest and most expensive. Will need regular plumping.

FEATHER CUSHIONS

When making feather cushion pads, channelled cushions should be made to help prevent the feathers from moving to the outer edges when sat on. They should be made from cambric or down-proof ticking. When using feather pads, always make the pad 2.5 cm (1 in) bigger all round than the finished cover size so that the pad fills the cushion cover, giving a well-plumped appearance.

FOAM AND POLYESTER WRAPS

When making foam cushions, cut the foam to size. Add a layer of at least 4 oz polyester, fixed with spray adhesive to the top and bottom and then cover the whole cushion, including the sides, with another layer of 4 oz polyester. Cover in stockinet to help ease the cushion pad into the cushion cover.

When cutting out the cushion cover fabric, cut the fabric to the size of the foam, excluding any polyester wrap etc. plus a 1.5 cm (⅝ in) seam allowance. Then when you sew the pieces together, the polyester will produce a snug fit.

PIPED SCATTER CUSHIONS

These are the easiest of cushion covers to make. Generally square or oblong in shape, they can be made quite simply in any fabric or, for those more adventurous, try manipulating the fabrics before stitching the two sides together. The combinations are endless:

- Panelling different fabrics together.
- Decorative techniques: quilting, ruching, appliqué, smocking, pleating.
- Borders: shaped and/or contrast.
- Trimmings: piping, fringes, cords, braids, ribbons, tassels.

TO MAKE

1 Measure the size of your cushion pad.

2 When re-using old pads, cut out two pieces of fabric the same size as the pad. When made up the cushion cover will be 3 cm (1¼ in) smaller but the pad will fill the cushion cover well, making it look more sumptuous. New pads will need a 1.5 cm (½ in) seam allowance all round.

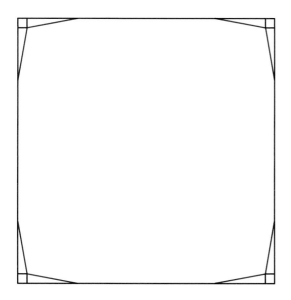

3 To help avoid 'dog ears' when you turn the fabric through to the right sides, taper the corners slightly: measure 1 cm (⅜ in) down from the corner and then draw a line to the adjacent side, a quarter of the width of the cushion. Do this on both sides of all the corners.

4 Overlock or zigzag stitch to neaten all the edges on both sides of the cushion.

5 Make and attach piping to one side of the cushion. See Piping on pages 52–3.

6 Pin the two pieces together and machine stitch in place, leaving one side open to insert the cushion pad. Turn through to the right side and insert the cushion pad.

7 Turn the raw edge in 1.5 cm (½ in) and slip stitch the opening closed. See Zips on pages 48–9 for various forms of zip insertion.

TIP Scatter cushions can be so simple and cheap to make that I often don't put zips in them. Zips are only necessary if you want to wash the cushion covers. So, unless you have spent a lot of money or time and effort in the making of your cushion cover, why waste time or money on inserting a zip? Just make another cover. That way you can change your accent colours quickly and easily.

BOX CUSHIONS

Box cushions are those with a border, used for seat or back cushions on chairs or window seats. I prefer to have seams at the corners, particularly if the cushion pad is made of foam as the seam will help keep the corners square.

1 Measure the cushion pad and make a cutting plan. See Cutting plan on page 39.

2 Mark and cut out the fabric pieces, taking into account any pattern matching required:
- Cut the top and bottom pieces with a 1.5 cm (⅝ in) seam allowance all round, i.e. 50 x 50 cm (18 x 18 in) = 53 x 53 cm (19 x 19 in).
- Cut the front and side border pieces with a 1.5 cm (⅝ in) seam allowance all round, i.e. 50 x 10 cm (18 x 4 in) = 53 x 13 cm (19 x 5 in).
- Cut two back zip border pieces (allow an extra 1.5 cm (⅝ in) to each piece to allow for the zip), i.e. 2 x 53 cm x 8 cm (2 x 19 x 3 in).

3 Overlock or zigzag stitch to neaten all the raw edges. Cut out and make up the piping.

4 Insert the zip in the back border. See Centred zip insertion on page 48.

5 Attach the piping to the top and bottom cushion pieces. See Piping on pages 52–3.

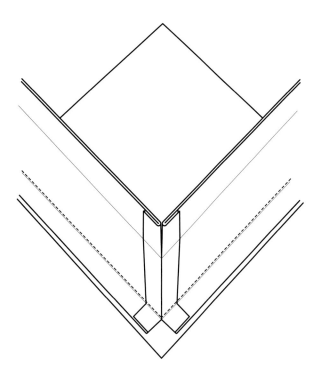

TIP When attaching a piece of fabric to a piped piece, the piped edge will always be tighter than the other and you will need to ease in any fullness. Therefore, pin the corners first, making sure the raw edges are level at each end. Pull the two pieces taut and pin the centre. Now working between the centre point and one end, pull the two pieces taut again, and pin that centre. Continue to pin in this way to ease in any fullness evenly.

6 Join the border pieces together. Leave 1 cm (⅜ in) unstitched at the top and bottom of each corner seam to allow the seam to ease around the corners. Open the zip slightly before attaching the top and bottom pieces to the border.

7 Pin the border to the cushion top and bottom, matching the corners and any pattern as required.

8 Machine stitch the pieces together. Check the fit and adjust as necessary. Fit the cushion pad.

PIPED BOLSTER CUSHIONS

Bolster cushions are cylindrical in shape with a standard size of approximately 18 cm (7 in) diameter by 45 cm (18 in) long, but they can be much larger.

The same process is used when making circular cushions with a small border.

1 Measure the bolster pad: its diameter and length. Calculate the circumference: multiply the diameter by 3.14 and then add 3 cm (1¼ in) seam allowances. Make a paper template of the circular end (diameter + 3 cm (1¼ in) seam allowance).

> *Cut out:*
> - 2 end circles
> - 1 x body (the circumference x length of the bolster + 3 cm (1¼ in) seam allowances)
> - Piping to go around each end
>
> i.e. for a 20 cm (8 in) diameter bolster:
>
> - 2 circular ends: 20 cm (8 in) + 3 cm (1¼ in) S/A = 23 cm (9 in) diameter
> - 1 body: 20 cm (8 in) x 3.14 = 63 cm (25 in) + 3 cm (1¼ in) S/A = 66 cm (26 in) (Circumference x length of bolster required plus 3 cm (1¼ in) seam allowances.)

2 Divide the end circles into four and mark with notches.

3 Make and attach the piping to the outside edge of the end circles. See Piping on pages 52–3.

4 Stitch in from each end of the body and insert the zip. Leave the zip open for turning through. See Zips on pages 48–9.

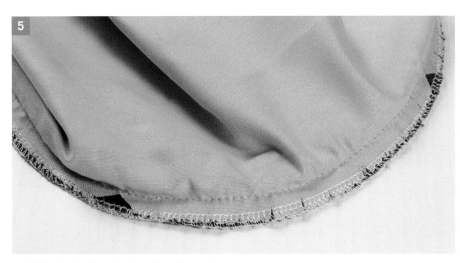

5

5 Divide the body end edges into four and mark with notches. Attach the body to the circular ends, matching the notches. Machine stitch in place.

6 Turn the fabric through to the right side and insert the cushion pad.

TIP When making cushion covers, the raw edges should always be neatened by overlocking or zigzag machining. This is particularly important if a cushion cover is to be washed. Zips do not necessarily mean that a cushion cover can be washed. In seat covers, the zip is often only there to aid the insertion of a foam pad.

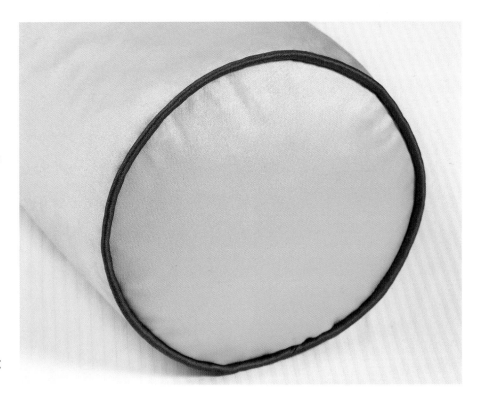

Lined curtains

Tie-backs

Interlined curtains

PROJECTS

Scatter cushions

Loose cover for an upright chair

Roman blind

Bed throw and valance

Window seat box and bolster cushions

LINED CURTAINS
WITH A COMMERCIAL HEADING TAPE

This window treatment is for a bedroom with a window that will have a functioning roman blind with dress-curtains and a firm pelmet above. The curtains are just for show; they are simple lined curtains with a standard 7.5 cm (3 in) pencil pleat heading.

Measure the window and complete the measuring chart on page 39:
- Track length: 134 cm (53 in)
- Finished drop of curtains: 225 cm (89 in)

Calculate and cut out the fabric requirements:
- Width: 134 cm x 2.5 = 335 cm divided by 137 cm = 2.45 rounded up to 3 widths
(Width: 53 in x 2.5 = 132½ in divided by 54 in = 2.45 rounded up to 3 widths)
- Drop: 225 cm + 25 cm heading and hem = 250 cm divided by the pattern repeat of 68 cm = 4 pattern repeats, i.e. 4 x 68 cm = 272 cm x 3 widths = 8.2 metres

(Drop: 89 in + 10 in heading and hem = 99 in divided by the pattern repeat of 27 in = 4 pattern repeats, i.e. 4 x 27 in = 108 in x 3 widths = 9 yards)

Material requirements:
- Main fabric: 8.2 metres (9 yards)
- Lining fabric: 8.2 metres (9 yards)
- Heading tape: 4.2 metres (4½ yards)
- 2 cord pockets
- 6 corner weights
- Thread
- Plastic pin hooks

1 Cut out the required drops of main fabric taking into account any pattern repeats. Add an extra 20 cm (8 in) for the hem and 5 cm (2 in) for the heading turning.

2 Cut the same amount of lining fabric. Join the widths of lining together and press the seams flat. Turn up a double 7 cm (2¾ in) hem and machine stitch in place close to the folded edge. Press and put to one side.

3 Join the widths of fabric together, pattern matching and pressing the seams as required.

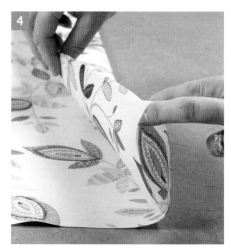

4 With rights sides of the fabric down, turn up a double 10 cm (4 in) hem and pin in place.

5 Turn the side in 5 cm (2 in) and pin in place.

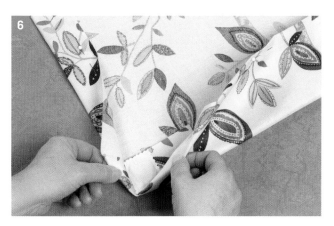

6 Mitre the corners and stitch corner weights into the corners and at the base of the joins.

7 Serge stitch the side turnings, using a stitch length of 5 cm (2 in).

8 Slip stitch the mitres, using a stitch length of 6 mm (¼ in).

9 Using a hand-stitched blind hem stitch, stitch the hem in place.

10 Lay the lining fabric on top of the curtain fabric, wrong sides together. Position the hem 3 cm (1¼ in) up from the bottom edge of the curtain.

11 Fold the lining fabric back and lock stitch the lining fabric to the curtain fabric, every third of a width. Make sure you match the colour of the thread to the curtain fabric.

12 Turn under the sides of the lining, 3 cm (1¼ in) from the outside edge and pin in place. Note: the corners of the lining should now be in line with the mitred corner of the curtain fabric.

13 Slip stitch the lining fabric to the curtain fabric, using a stitch length of 1.5 cm (⅝ in).

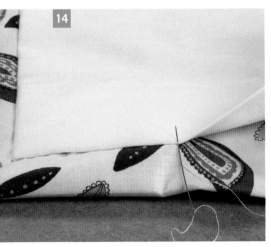

14 Reduce the length of the stitch to 6 mm (¼ in) and slip stitch 10 cm (4 in) along the bottom edge of the lining, securing the ends firmly.

15 Make and fit a chain bar every half width and at the joins in the fabric.

16 Measuring from the bottom edge of the curtain, mark the finished drop point with pins.

17 Measure 5 cm (2 in) from the finished drop point and cut off any excess fabric. Turn the top of the fabric down at the finished drop point and pin in place.

18 Cover the raw edges with the pencil pleat tape positioned 6 mm (¼ in) down from the top edge.

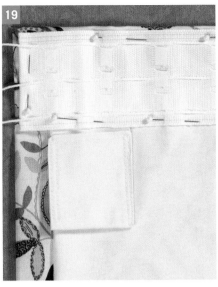

19 Insert a cord pocket under the bottom edge of the heading tape in line with the edge of the lining fabric.

20 Machine stitch the tape in place, stitching close to the edges.

21 Pull up the cords to the required width of the curtain plus 4 cm (1½ in) to allow for spring-back.

22 Fit plastic curtain hooks into the tape every 10 cm (4 in) along the heading tape. Hang and dress the curtains into neat folds.

TIP When dressing curtains, push the curtain fabric back between the hooks and run your hands down the length of the curtain to form neat folds. If necessary, tie the folds in place using offcuts of fabric, leaving them in place for as long as possible to set the folds.

TIE-BACKS
WITH CONTRAST PIPED EDGE

The curtains will then have matching tie-backs with a contrast piped edge. Once the curtains have been hung you can measure the embrace of the curtains using a soft tape measure. This will give you the correct size tie-back for the amount of fabric used in the curtain.

Material requirements:
- Tie-back buckram 30 cm (12 in) wide x 1.5 metre (1½ yards)
- Polyester wadding: 1 metre (1 yard)
- Main fabric: 1 metre (1 yard)
- Lining: 1 metre (1 yard)
- Contrast fabric for piping: 30 cm (12 in)
- Piping cord: 4 metres (4⅓ yards)
- 4 brass 'D' rings
- Thread

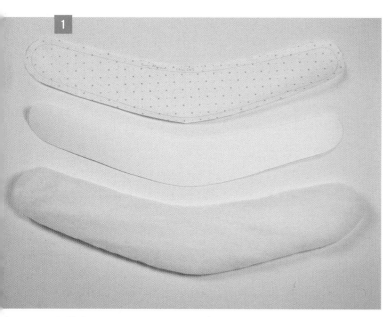

1 Make a paper pattern of the tie-back shape to be used. In this case I am using a banana shaped tie-back. Cut two shapes out of tie-back/pelmet buckram and cover with 8 oz polyester wadding.

2 Position the fabric's pattern on the tie-back. Don't forget there is a left- and a right-hand tie-back so the pattern should be positioned accordingly.

5 Join the two ends of the piping neatly. See Joining piping on page 53.

6 With right sides together, pin the lining to the tie-back fabric and machine stitch around the tie-back again. Leave a gap at the bottom edge, large enough to insert the wadded buckram.

7 Snip around the curves and turn the tie-back through to the right side. Press as required.

8 Insert the wadded buckram, making sure the seam allowance is positioned at the back of the tie-back buckram.

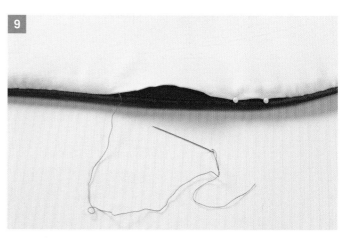

3 Mark and cut out the two tie-backs with a 1.5 cm (⅝ in) seam allowance all round. Make up enough contrast piping to go around each tie-back, i.e. approximately 4 metres (4⅓ yards).

4 With the raw edges together, stitch the piping to the right side of the tie-back fabric. Snip into the piping to ease it around the curves.

9 Turn in the seam allowance and slip stitch the bottom edge closed.

10 Attach brass rings, using a buttonhole stitch. The front ring should be level with the edge of the tie-back and the back ring should be placed half over the edge to allow it to catch the tie-back hook on the wall.

INTERLINED CURTAINS

This living room is decorated in neutral tones with the curtains providing the accent colour at these large patio doors. The curtains are interlined to enhance the drape of the fabric, as well as their insulating properties. An added contrast leading edge and triple pleats with contrast inserts and buttons add to the decorative detailing.

Measure the window and complete the measuring chart on page 39:
- Track length: 300 cm (117 in)
- Finished drop of curtains: 237 cm (94 in)

Calculate and cut out the fabric requirements:
- Width: 300 cm x 2.25 = 675 cm divided by 137 cm = 4.93 rounded up to 5 widths

(Width: 117 in x 2.25 = 263 in divided by 54 in = 4.87 rounded up to 5 widths)

- Drop: 237 cm + 30 cm heading and hem = 267 cm divided by the pattern repeat of 64 cm = 5 pattern repeats, i.e. 5 x 64 cm = 320 cm x 5 widths = 16 metres

(Drop: 94 in + 12 in heading and hem = 106 in divided by the pattern repeat of 25 in = 5 pattern repeats, i.e. 5 x 25 in = 125 in x 5 widths = 17⅓ yards)

Material requirements:
- Main fabric: 16 metres (17⅓ yards)
- Contrast fabric: 2.8 metres (3 yards)
- Lining fabric: 16 metres (17⅓ yards)
- Interlining: 18.8 metres (20 yards)
- Heading buckram: 7 metres (7⅔ yards)
- 10 corner weights
- Thread
- Pin hooks
- 20 covered buttons

1 Cut out the required drops of main fabric taking into account any pattern repeats. Pattern match the fabric and join the lengths together. Press the seams flat.

2 Cut two pieces of contrast fabric 25 cm (10 in) wide for the leading edge and attach to the leading edge of each curtain.

3 Cut out and join together the lengths of lining.

4 Cut out the lengths of interlining. The interlining will need to be 30 cm (12 in) wider than the finished widths of the fabric.

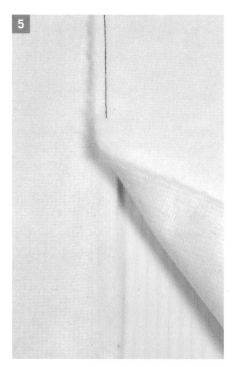

5 Join together the lengths of interlining using a single lapped seam to avoid bulk.

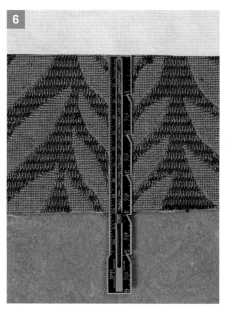

6 Position the interlining 10 cm (4 in) up from the bottom edge of the curtain and lock stitch in place every ⅓ of a width. Also lock stitch the interlining to the seam where the main fabric joins the contrast fabric.

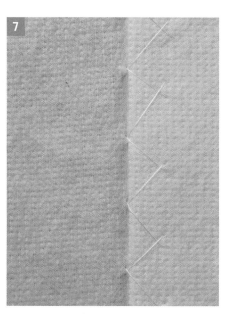

7 Fold the leading edge of the interlining in a double 10 cm (4 in) to form three layers of interlining 10 cm (4 in) wide. Herringbone stitch in place.

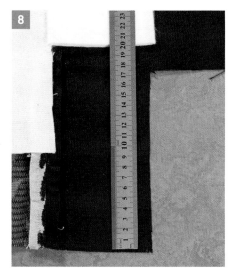

8 Cut out the excess interlining at the bottom of the leading edge, in line with the hem of the curtain, i.e. 20 cm (8 in) up from the bottom of the fabric.

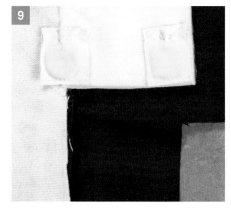

9 Place weights in the leading edge corner and at the base of all joins.

10 Fold over the leading edge fabric and pin in place.

11 Turn up a double 10 cm (4 in) hem and pin in place.

12 Turn in the back edge of the curtain 5 cm (2 in) and pin. Serge stitch in place.

13 Mitre the back edge corner and insert a corner weight. Slip stitch closed.

14 Herringbone stitch the hem and the contrast leading edge to the interlining.

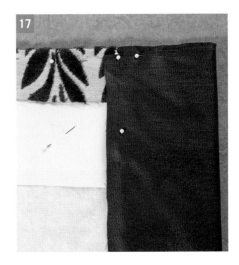

17 Insert heading buckram along the top edge and pin in place. Turn the fabric down, cutting off any excess fabric that may show below the buckram. Pin in place.

15 Turn under the bottom edges of the leading edge, cutting out any excess fabric as necessary. Slip stitch in place.

18 Position the lining fabric 3 cm (1¼ in) up from the bottom edge. Turn the lining fabric back and lock stitch in place every ⅓ of a width. Turn the back edge lining fabric in 3 cm (1¼ in) and slip stitch in place down the back edge and 10 cm (4 in) in along the bottom edge of the lining.

16 Measure and mark the finished drop point with pins and cut off any excess interlining at this point.

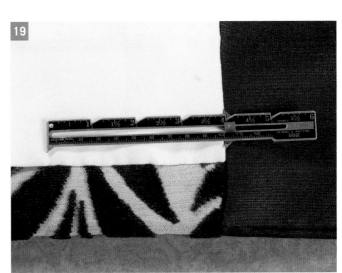

19 Turn the lining under at the leading edge, cutting off any excess fabric as required, and slip stitch in place down the front edge and 10 cm (4 in) in along the bottom edge.

20 Turn the lining under at the top edge, cutting off any excess fabric as required. Slip stitch in place, leaving the pins to hold the buckram in place whilst you work the heading pleats.

21 Calculate the triple pleat spacings and mark their position with pins.

22 Pin the pleats in place and machine stitch the back of each pleat.

23 Cut out the contrast fabric for the pleat inserts: 18 cm (7 in) deep x ⅓ the width of each pleat. Turn under 1.5 cm (⅝ in) all round and iron in place.

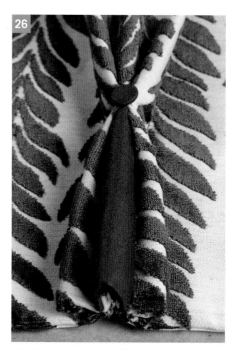

24 Pin the contrast fabric inserts over the centre section of the triple pleats and slip stitch in place.

25 Form the triple pleats and over-sew in place.

26 Make contrast fabric buttons and stitch to the bottom of each pleat.

27 Fit pin hooks into the back of each pleat. Hang and dress in the curtains.

ROMAN BLIND
WITH A CONTRAST PANEL AND BEADED TRIM

This blind is fitted inside the window recess and is attached to a wooden batten with a depth of 5 cm (2 in). The blind is made using eyelets and china cord guides.

Measure the window and complete the measuring chart on page 39:
- Top, middle and bottom, as well as left, right and centre. 132 cm (52 in) drop x 104 cm (41 in) wide.

Material requirements:
- Main fabric: 1.6 metres (63 in)
- Contrast fabric: 10 cm (4 in)
- Lining fabric: 1.6 metres (63 in)
- Domette interlining: 1.3 metres (51 in)
- Beaded trim: 1.2 metres (47 in)
- Velcro: 1.1 metres (43 in)
- 12 eyelets
- Rods: 3 x 1.02 metres (40 in)
- Weight: 1 x 1.02 metres (40 in)
- Wooden batten: 104 cm (41 in)
- 4 china guides
- 1 brass weight
- Roman blind cord: 9 metres (10 yards)
- Thread

Calculate and cut out the fabric requirements:
Main fabric:
- Finished drop of the blind: 132 cm (52 in) + 10 cm (4 in) for the hem and top allowances = 142 cm (56 in)
- Finished width of blind: 104 cm (41 in) + 8 cm (3 in) for turnings = 112 cm (44 in)

- Facing: finished width plus turnings: 112 cm (44 in) x 11.5 cm (4½ in) deep

Lining fabric:
- Finished drop of the blind: 132 cm (52 in) + 10 cm (4 in) for the top and hem allowances + 12 cm (4½ in) for the rod pockets (i.e. 4 cm (1½ in) for each rod pocket
- Add an extra 2 cm (1 in) to the finished width of the blind, i.e. 106 cm (42 in)

Domette interlining:
- Finished depth of blind: 132 cm (52 in) x finished width of the blind: 104 cm (41 in)

Contrast panel:
- Finished width of the blind plus turnings: 112 cm (44 in) x 10 cm (4 in) deep

Beaded trim:
- Width of blind plus turnings: 112 cm (44 in)

Calculate the pleat dimensions:
- Measure the distance from the top of the wooden batten to the bottom of the cord guides: 5 cm (2 in)
- Deduct this measurement from the finished drop of the blind to give you the amount of fabric for the pleats:

132 cm – 5 cm = 127 cm (52 in – 2 in = 50 in)
- Divide this figure by the number of half-pleats required: 127 cm divided by 7 = 18 cm (50 in divided by 7 = 7 in)
- This will give you the depth of each half-pleat: 7 x 18 cm (7 in)
(See Pleat calculations on page 96.)

1 Measure 11.5 cm (4½ in) from the bottom edge of the blind fabric and attach the contrast fabric panel:

- Turn the top and bottom edges in to meet at the centre back of the panel and press in place. The panel should be 5 cm (2 in) deep.
- Position the contrast fabric on the blind and top stitch in place, stitching close to the edges.

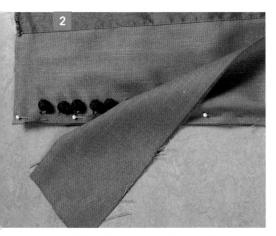

2 With right sides together, pin the bead trim to the bottom edge of the blind and cover with the facing fabric. Machine stitch together with a 1.5 cm (⅝ in) seam allowance, stitching as close to the beading as possible.

3 Lining fabric: turn the sides in 2.5 cm (1 in) and iron in place.

4 Turn the bottom hem up 4 cm (1½ in) to form the weight pocket and machine stitch close to the raw edge.

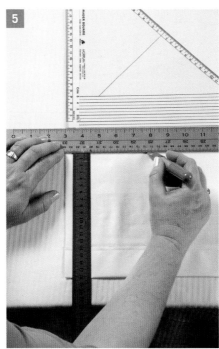

5 Working on the wrong side of the lining fabric, mark the position of the rod pockets. Each rod pocket should be 4 cm (1½ in) deep to allow for the eyelets.

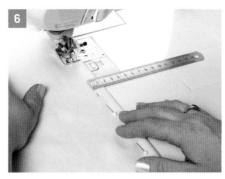

6 Pin and machine stitch the rod pockets in place, stitching 1.5 cm (⅝ in) from the folded edge.

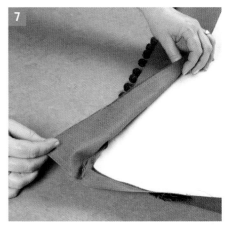

7 Lay the main fabric on the table with the wrong side up and place the domette interlining in the seam of the hem and centred from side to side. Make sure it is in line with the bottom edge of the blind.

8 Fold the interlining back and lock stitch in place horizontally every 30 cm (12 in) up the length of the blind.

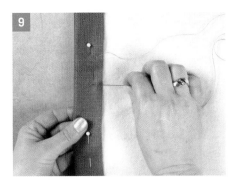

9　Turn in the sides of the blind 4 cm (1½ in) enclosing the domette and serge stitch close to the raw edges.

10　Herringbone stitch the interlining to the fabric at the top edge.

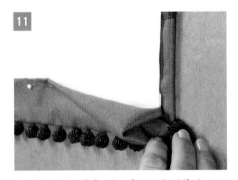

11　Place the lining fabric on the blind, centred from side to side, and tuck the bottom weight pocket neatly into the seam at the bottom of the blind. Turn the facing fabric to form a double 5 cm (2 in) hem and pin in place.

12　Quick mitre the ends of the hem so that they line up with the lining.

13　Carefully smooth the lining up the blind, pinning the rod pockets in place. Leave the top edge until last. Slip stitch the sides, closing one side of each rod pocket as you go. Slip stitch the hem and one end of the weight pocket.

14　As the interlining is the exact measurement of the finished blind, it should mark the position of the finished drop point of the blind. Check and pin the domette in place.

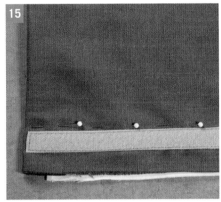

15　Turn the fabric over and attach the soft side of Velcro 6 mm (¼ in) above the finished drop point.

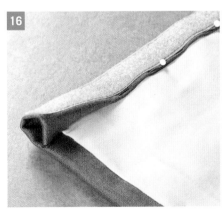

16　Turn the Velcro down and cutting off any excess fabric, turn the raw edges under. Slip stitch in place at the back of the blind.

17　Using the wooden batten as your guide, mark the position of the cords on the rod pockets, using a fine pencil or marker pen.

18　Stab stitch through all the layers of fabric at the top of each rod pocket in line with the cords. Following the eyelet instructions provided, use an eyelet machine or small eyelet kit, to fit the eyelets to each rod pocket in line with the cords.

19　Insert the rods and bottom weight into their appropriate pockets and slip stitch the ends closed.

20　Fit the blind to the wooden batten. See Track and batten systems for blinds on page 21.

21　Thread the cords through the eyelets, tying off with a slip knot on each of the bottom eyelets. Tension the cords and fit a brass weight to the other end of the cords to form the pull cord. Hang and dress the blind.

BED VALANCE

This fitted bed valance with contrast kick pleats on the sides and bottom corners is to go in the bedroom and will co-ordinate with the fabrics used on the roman blind.

Measure the bed base:
- Width: 90 cm (36 in)
- Length: 193 cm (76 in)
- Depth of base: 40 cm (16 in)
- Depth of skirt: 40 + 8 cm (16 + 3 in) for turnings. The skirt should finish 1.5 cm (⅝ in) off the floor.

Material requirements:
- Main fabric: 2.6 metres (102 in)
- Contrast fabric: 50 cm (½ yard)
- Sheeting: (240 cm / 94 in wide) x 1 metre (1¼ yards)
- Lining fabric: 3 metres (3 yards)
- Thread

Make a cutting plan:

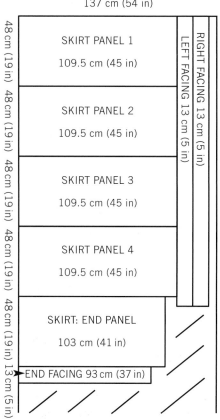

Cut out the various fabric pieces:
- Sheeting for the base: 90 cm + 3 cm S/A x 193 cm + 3 cm S/A
(Sheeting for base: 36 in + 1 in S/A x 76 in + 1 in S/A)
- Skirt sides: 4 x 96.5 cm + 10 cm for turnings = 106.5 cm wide x 40 cm + 5 cm for the hem + 3 cm S/A = 48 cm deep
(Skirt sides: 4 x 38 in + 4 in for turnings = 42 in wide x 16 in + 2 in for the hem + 1 in S/A = 19 in deep)
Skirt end: 1 x 90 cm + 10 cm for turnings = 100 cm wide x 40 cm + 5 cm for the hem + 3 cm S/A = 48 cm deep
(Skirt end: 1 x 36 in + 4 in for turnings = 40 in wide x 16 in + 2 in for the hem + 1 in S/A = 19 in deep)
- Skirt linings: width as per skirt measurements above. Depth is less 5 cm (2 in) for the hem.
- Side facings: 2 x 193 cm + 3 cm S/A = 196 cm long x 10 cm + 3 cm S/A wide
(Side facings: 2 x 76 in + 1 in S/A = 77 in long x 4 in + 1 in S/A wide)

- End facing: 1 x 90 cm + 3 cm S/A x 10 cm + 3 cm S/A
(End facing: 1 x 36 in + 1 in S/A x 4 in + 1 in S/A)
- Contrast kick pleats and linings: 4 x 20 cm + 3 cm S/A = 23 cm wide x 40 cm + 2.5 cm for the hem + 3 cm S/A = 45.5 cm deep
(Contrast kick pleats and linings: 4 x 8 in + 1 in S/A = 9 in wide x 16 in + 1 in for the hem + 1 in S/A = 18 in deep)

S/A = Seam Allowance

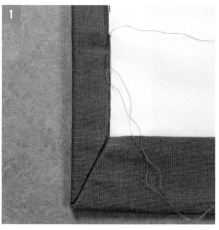

1 **Make up the five separate skirt panels. Stitch the lining to the bottom edge of each skirt panel, with a 1.5 cm (⅝ in) seam allowance. Leave 8 cm (3 in) free at each end. Turn the hem up 5 cm (2 in) and the sides in 5 cm (2 in) and quick mitre the corners. Turn the lining in 3 cm (1¼ in) from the outside edges, trimming any excess as required and slip stitch in place.**

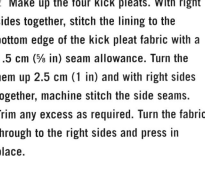

2 Make up the four kick pleats. With right sides together, stitch the lining to the bottom edge of the kick pleat fabric with a 1.5 cm (⅝ in) seam allowance. Turn the hem up 2.5 cm (1 in) and with right sides together, machine stitch the side seams. Trim any excess as required. Turn the fabric through to the right sides and press in place.

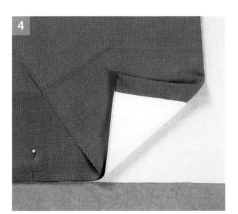

3 Position the skirt panels and kick pleats together in sequence. The kick pleats should be 1 cm (⅜ in) shorter than the skirt panels.

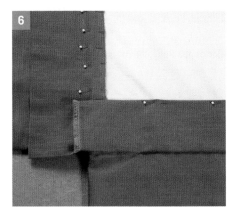

4 Place the skirt and kick pleat panels and the facing, with right sides together, on the wrong side of the sheeting.

5 Pin and machine stitch in place with a 1.5 cm (½ in) seam allowance.

6 With right sides of the fabric up, turn the raw edges of the facing under and pin in place.

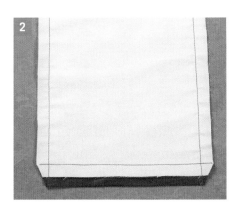

7 Mitre the bottom corners of the facing and top stitch in place. Top stitch close to the folded edge of the facing.

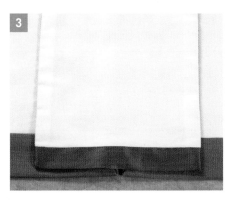

8 Turn under the raw edges at the top of the valance and machine stitch to neaten. Press and fit on the bed.

BED THROW

This bed throw is wadded with polyester to make it more sumptuous. I have patchworked together the various fabrics used on the other projects in the bedroom to form a contemporary geometric design, which could easily be enlarged for a larger bed.

1 Measure over any bedding to be used and make the throw slightly larger so that it covers all the bedding.

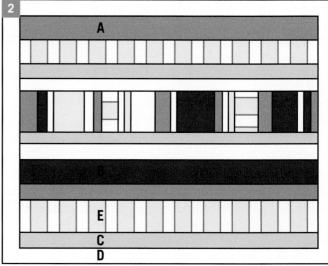

2 Make a scale drawing of your design, making a note of the measurements of the various pieces.

A = mauve

B = crimson

C = sage green

D = cream

E = striped fabric

3 Cut out all the fabric pieces for the small patchwork strip. Allow a 6 mm (¼ in) seam allowance all round.

4 Cut out all the fabric pieces for the long patchwork strips. Allow a 6 mm (¼ in) seam allowance on the long sides and a 1.5 cm (⅝ in) seam allowance at each end. The two outside strips will need a 1.5 cm (⅝ in) seam allowance on the outside edges in order to match up with the border's seam allowance.

5 Cut the four border pieces, twice their width by their depth, plus 1.5 cm (⅝ in) seam allowance all round.

Material requirements:
- Colours A, B, C and E: 2 metres (78 in) of each
- Colour D: 2.2 metres (86 in)
- Sheeting: 1.7 metres (67 in)
- 5 oz polyester wadding: 3.4 metres (133 in)
- Thread

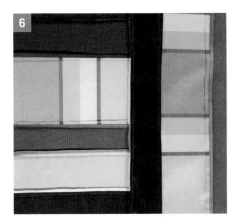

6 Stitch the small patchwork pieces together with a 6 mm (¼ in) seam allowance to form a long strip of horizontal stripes. Press the seams flat. Stitch all the long strips together in sequence, with a 6 mm (¼ in) seam allowance to form the large central panel of patchwork. Press all the seams flat.

7 Check the overall dimensions of the panel and adjust as necessary. You will need to be accurate in order to fit the double mitred border.

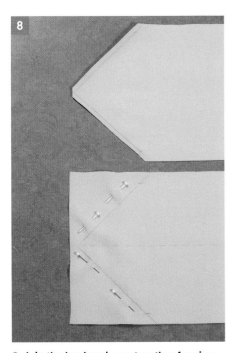

8 Join the border pieces together forming double mitred corners.

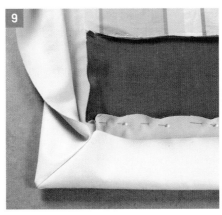

9 Pin and stitch the border to the central patchwork panel with a 1.5 cm (⅝ in) seam allowance.

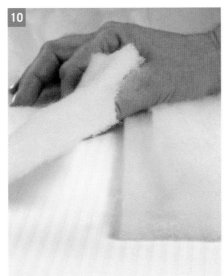

10 Place 5 oz polyester wadding, cut to the finished size of the throw, on the wrong sides of the fabric. Note: If you need to join the polyester, step the join and hand stitch together with a single lapped seam to avoid bulk.

11 Lock stitch the polyester to the seams of the patchwork.

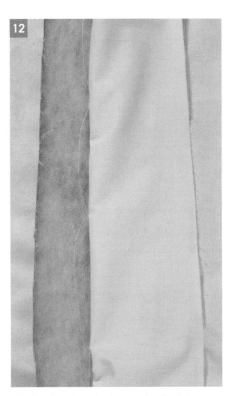

12 Cut the sheeting for the back of the throw to size. Place the sheeting over the back of the throw and lock stitch in place to the polyester.

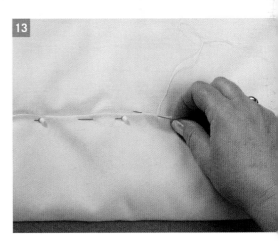

13 Enclose the raw edges of the sheeting inside the border. Turn under the border's raw edges 1.5 cm (⅝ in) and slip stitch to the sheeting to neaten.

WINDOW SEAT BOX AND BOLSTER CUSHIONS

In order to make good-looking box cushions you will need to be accurate in your measurements, machining and fitting. Take your time to match up large patterns. If you have a small pattern repeat, it may be better to centre the pattern top to bottom of the border. Stripes should run in line over the top of the cushion down the front and under the seat, but if your fabric has an asymmetric design, you will not be able to pattern match them on the underside. Stripes and patterns on borders should always run down the depth, not the length, of the border.

WINDOW SEAT BOX CUSHION

These cushions are to go on a large box positioned under a window to form an additional seating area. The box measures 128 cm (50 in) long by 46 cm (18 in) deep.

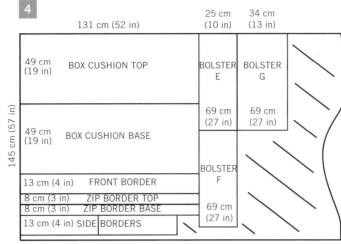

4 Mark and cut out all the fabric pieces and overlock or zigzag to neaten all the raw edges.

Material requirements:
- Main fabric: 1.4 metres (55 in)
- Contrast piping fabric: 30 cm (12 in)
- Piping cord: 7.5 metres (8 yards)
- Continuous zip: 1.3 metres (51 in)
- Velcro: 1.3 metres (51 in)
- Thread
- Foam cushion pad

5 Cut out and make up the contrast piping. Stitch the contrast piping to the top and bottom cushion pieces. Make the joins on the sides of the cushion.

1 Take the measurements of the window seat base.

2 Make or have made a foam cushion pad with a polyester wrap and stockinet: 128 cm long (50 in) x 46 cm (18 in) deep with a 10 cm (4 in) border.

3 Make a cutting plan, including seam allowances of 1.5 cm (⅝ in) all round. Note: this fabric is railroad.

6 Stitch the soft side of Velcro to the bottom fabric, 15 cm (6 in) from the back edge. The hook side will be attached to the top of the window seat to stop the cushion from slipping.

7 Fit a continuous zip in the centre of the back border piece.

8 Join the front and side border pieces together, with seams at the corners to help stop the corners from pulling in and rounding.

9 Join the zip border to the side border pieces. Leave the zip partially open for turning through.

10 Pin the border to the cushion top, lining up the corners and the stripes, and easing in any fullness. Machine stitch in place.

11 Pin the other side of the cushion to the border in the same way and machine stitch together. Fit the foam cushion pad to check the fit and adjust as necessary.

BOLSTER CUSHION

This bolster cushion is longer than usual and is being made to fit along the back edge of the box cushion. A pad of this size would need to be made-to-measure. As it is a long cushion, some decorative panels have been incorporated to break up its length and the ends have been pleated with alternating fabrics.

Material requirements:
- Main fabric: 60 cm (24 in)
- Green contrast fabric: 50 cm (20 in)
- Brown contrast fabric: 50 cm (20 in)
- Lining fabric: 25 cm (10 in)
- Concealed zips: 2 x 55 cm (22 in)
- Piping cord No.1: 1.4 metres (55 in)
- Piping cord No.3: 1.4 metres (55 in)
- 2 rosettes
- Thread

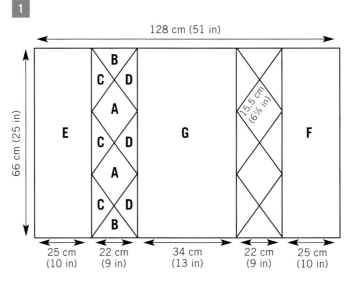

1 Measure the window seat and make a scale drawing of your chosen design.

Add the appropriate seam allowances:
- **Length: 128 cm + 3 cm S/A = 131 cm (51 in + 1 in S/A = 52 in)**
- **Diameter: 21 cm + 3 cm S/A = 24 cm (8 in + 1 in S/A = 9 in)**
- **Circumference: 21 cm x 3.14 = 66 cm + 3 cm S/A = 69 cm (8 in x 3.14 = 25 in + 1 in S/A = 27 in)**

2 **Make paper templates of the bolster ends, the pleat segments, the decorative diamond and triangular shapes. Cut out with a 1.5 cm (⅝ in) seam allowance all round.**

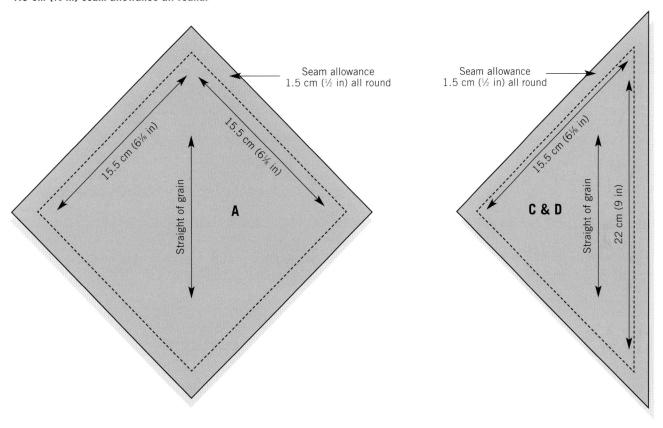

Seam allowance 1.5 cm (½ in) all round

15.5 cm (6⅛ in)

15.5 cm (6⅛ in)

Straight of grain

A

Seam allowance 1.5 cm (½ in) all round

15.5 cm (6⅛ in)

22 cm (9 in)

Straight of grain

C & D

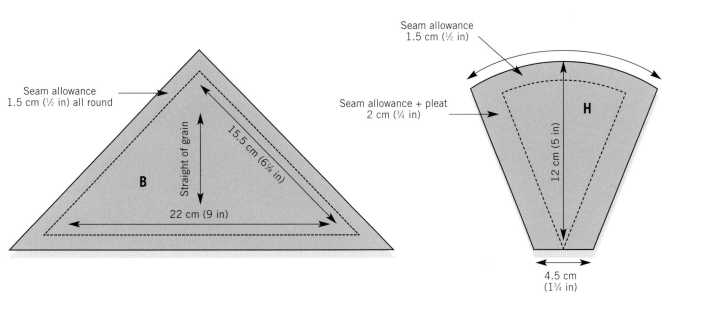

Seam allowance 1.5 cm (½ in) all round

Straight of grain

15.5 cm (6⅛ in)

B

22 cm (9 in)

Seam allowance 1.5 cm (½ in)

Seam allowance + pleat 2 cm (¾ in)

12 cm (5 in)

H

4.5 cm (1¾ in)

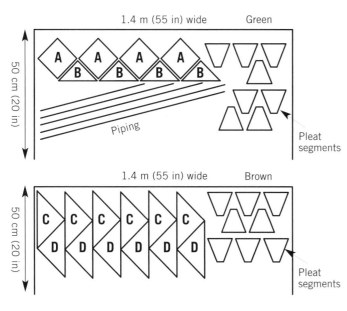

1.4 m (55 in) wide   Green

50 cm (20 in)

A A A A

B B B B

Piping

Pleat segments

1.4 m (55 in) wide   Brown

50 cm (20 in)

C C C C C C

D D D D D D

Pleat segments

3 Make cutting plans of the different fabrics. Also see the Box cushion cutting plan on page 141.

4 Mark and cut out all the fabric pieces with a 1.5 cm (⅝ in) seam allowance.

5 Cut two circular ends out of lining fabric to use as foundations for the pleated ends.

6 Cut out and make up the different sized piping cords: 1.4 metres (55 in) of each No. 1 and No. 3.

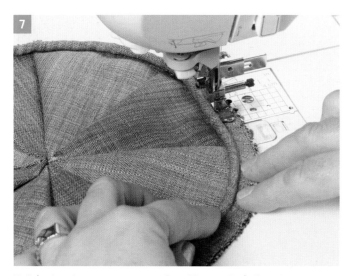

7 Join the pleat segments together. Pleat and stitch to the foundation lining to form the bolster ends. Attach the contrast piping to the bolster ends.

8 Cover the raw edges in the centre of the bolster ends with a rosette and stitch in place.

9 Join the diamond and triangular shaped pieces together to form the decorative panels. Attach the No.1 shoestring piping cord to the edges of these decorative panels. Use the zip foot to stitch as close as possible to the piping, machining in one direction only.

10 Attach the main fabric pieces and the decorative panels together to form the body of the bolster cushion.

12 Fit the pleated bolster ends and the main body pieces together, and machine stitch in place with a 1.5 cm (⅝ in) seam allowance.

11 Matching the stripes and the decorative panels, insert concealed zips, stitching any excess seam together at each end. As concealed zips only come in standard lengths to a maximum of 55 cm (22 in), fit two zips together closing in the centre. See Concealed zip insertion on page 49.

13 Turn through to the right sides and insert the feather cushion pad. Check the fit and adjust as necessary.

SCATTER CUSHIONS

Using the three different fabrics used on the box and bolster cushions, I have made a range of scatter cushions using the different methods of zip insertion and decorative techniques described earlier in this book.

TIP Don't forget that when you fit a zip in the centre of a panel, you may need to pattern match the fabric and to add a 1.5 cm (⅝ in) seam allowance to each side of the zip.

SCATTER CUSHION WITH RUCHED PIPING

This is a simple square scatter cushion enhanced with a ruched piped edge and fitted with a concealed zip in the back.

Material requirements:
- Cushion pad: 46 x 46 cm (18 x 18 in)
- Main fabric: 50 cm (20 in)
- Contrast fabric: 30 cm (12 in) to make 4 metres (156 in) in length of piping
- Piping cord: 4 m (156 in)
- Concealed zip: 46 cm (18 in)
- Thread

1 Make as per Piped scatter cushion (see pages 118–19), but ruche the fabric onto the piping instead of making plain piping. See ruched piping on page 59.

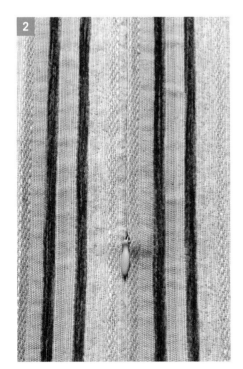

2 Fit a concealed zip into the back of the cushion. See Concealed zip insertion on page 49.

SCATTER CUSHION WITH QUILTED PANELS

This rectangular cushion has a front with two different quilted effects, trimmed with a decorative trimming and a plain back with a centred zip.

Material requirements:
- Cushion pad: 40 x 50 cm (16 x 20 in)
- Striped fabric: 50 cm (20 in)
- Green fabric for quilting: 50 cm (20 in)
- Brown fabric for twin needle quilting: 50 cm (20 in)
- Piping cord: 2 m (78 in)
- Continuous zip: 40 cm (16 in)
- Braid: 50 cm (20 in)
- Thread

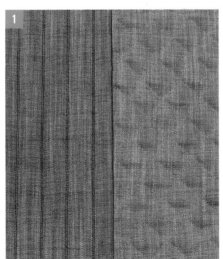

1 Make up the quilted sections that form the front panels: brown fabric with twin needle quilting and green fabric with a diamond quilting effect. See Quilting on pages 65–7. Cut the quilted sections to size and machine together.

2 Stitch the trimming over the seam.

3 Fit a centred zip in the centre of the striped back panel. See Centred zip insertion on page 48. Make up and attach the piping to the back panel.

4 Machine stitch the front and back cushion panels together.

SCATTER CUSHION WITH TUCKS AND KNIFE-PLEATED FRILL

This rectangular cushion has a front with cross tucks and pin tucks trimmed with braid, and a knife pleated frill, fitted with a lapped zip in the bottom edge.

Material requirements:
- Cushion pad: 40 x 50 cm (16 x 20 in)
- Striped fabric: 50 cm (20 in)
- Green fabric for pleats and tucks: 1 m (1 yard)
- Continuous zip: 40 cm (16 in)
- Braid: 50 cm (20 in)
- Thread

1 Make up the cross tucks and pin tuck panels and machine stitch together to form the cushion's front panel. See Tucks on pages 57–8.

2 Slip stitch the braid over the joining seam.

3 Make up the knife pleat frill and attach it to the front panel. See Pleats on pages 55–6.

4 Fit a lapped zip in the bottom edge of the cushion and machine stitch the front and back panels together. See Lapped zip insertion on page 49.

SCATTER CUSHION WITH MINI TUCKS

This square cushion has mini tucks on the front and a centred lapped zip in the back.

Material requirements:
- Cushion pad: 46 x 46 cm (18 x 18 in)
- Striped fabric: 60 cm (24 in)
- Brown fabric: 50 cm (20 in)
- Piping cord: 2 m (2 yards)
- Continuous zip: 50 cm (20 in)
- Thread

1 Make up the mini tuck front panel. See Tucks on pages 57–8.

2 Fit the lapped zip in the centre of the back panel. Make up and attach the piping to the back panel.

3 Pin and stitch the front and back panels together.

LOOSE COVERS

The purpose of loose covers is to protect the original upholstery. Alternatively, they are designed to cover old upholstery and to breathe new life into chairs that have seen better days. They should be tailored to fit to give the appearance of fitted upholstery, but loose enough to be easily removed but they should never be baggy.

Before you embark on the making of a loose cover consider these points:

- Loose covers are not necessarily a cheap option to re-upholstery. Often, there is as much work in a loose cover as there is in the recovering of a chair. The only difference is that you will get a better finish from recovering where the fabrics can be pulled taut and secured in place.
- Do you want to wash the cover regularly? If so, choose the fabric with care. Many of today's fabrics have a mix of fibre compositions or special treatments applied to them that make washing inadvisable, as once washed, they either shrink or look lifeless.
- Natural fibre fabrics are your best option but, beware, natural fibres have a tendency to shrink. Therefore, either wash the fabric before you make the cover, make the cover slightly larger to allow for shrinkage or make it to fit properly and if it shrinks, make a replacement.
- In the UK, fabrics must comply with the Fire Regulations (see page 156).

CHOICE OF COVERS

It is essential to choose the right type of fabric for making loose covers. The fabric must be hard-wearing to withstand 'bums on seats' and laundering, and should be shrink- and fade-resistant. Choose a fabric that is firm, smooth and closely woven. Loosely woven fabrics are not suitable as they loose their shape quickly and do not wear well.

Piping will define the outline of the chair as well as strengthening the seams, giving a more professional finish. The fabric used for piping can be the same or a contrasting fabric but, ideally, should be of a similar weight to the main fabric. Natural piping cords will shrink, so if you need to use it you should pre-shrink it before use by pouring boiling water over the cord and letting it dry. Remember to cut more than is required to allow for shrinkage.

MEASURING FOR LOOSE COVERS

When taking measurements for loose covers always measure the widest part of the chair. Remember that the legs are often shaped so can be wider at the knee or the base, with back legs tapering out at the bottom. Take this into account when deciding on the shape and style of any skirt to be fitted.

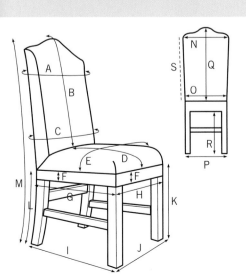

A - Inside back top width = 62 cm (24½ in)
B - Inside back depth plus tuck-in allowance = 79 cm (31 in)
C - Inside back base width = 66 cm (26 in)
D - Seat length plus tuck-in allowance = 56 cm (22 in)
E - Seat width = 60 cm (23½ in)
F - Seat depth (front) = 12 cm (5 in)
F - Seat depth (sides) = 12 cm (5 in)
G - Width of sides at top of legs = 54 cm (21 in)
H - Width of front at top of legs = 57 cm (22½ in)

I - Width of sides at base of legs = 57 cm (22½ in)
J - Width of front at base of legs = 57 cm (22½ in)
K - Height of front legs = 37 cm (14½ in)
L - Height of back legs = 37 cm (14½ in)
M - Height of back = 114 cm (45 in)
N - Width of outside back at top = 47 cm (18½ in)
O - Width of outside back at base = 47 cm (18½ in)
P - Width of back at base of legs = 47 cm (18½ in)
Q - Length of outside back = 77 cm (30½ in)
R - Length of back legs = 37 cm (14½ in)
S - Length of opening, if required

LOOSE COVER FOR AN UPRIGHT CHAIR

This project is an example of where the fabric's pattern can have a dramatic effect on the design of a piece. This fabric has a leaf design that flows in waves down its length. The original design was to have a central box pleat in the back, but the straight lines of the centre pleat with the curving design of the fabric made it look as if the fabric has been put on off-centre. Therefore, the design of the loose cover was modified to incorporate two back corner pleats that show the fabric's design at its best.

Material requirements:
- Main fabric: 3.4 metres (133 in)
- Contrast fabric: 1.3 metres (51 in)
- Lining fabric: 2.5 metres (98 in)
- Piping cord: 4.4 metres (172 in)
- Thread

1 Take accurate measurements of the chair and make a cutting plan adding 2.5 cm (1 in) for seam allowances, and 5 cm (2 in) for hems and the tuck-in. Cut out and identify the various fabric pieces.

Pattern repeat (PR) = 68 cm (27 in)

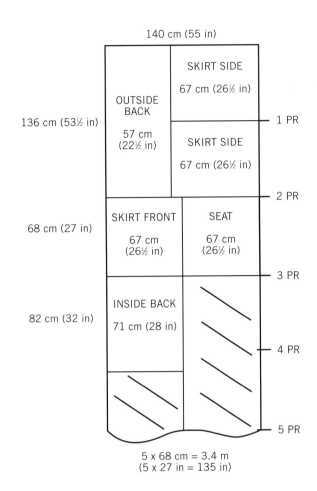

140 cm (55 in)

OUTSIDE BACK 57 cm (22½ in)	SKIRT SIDE 67 cm (26½ in)
	SKIRT SIDE 67 cm (26½ in)

136 cm (53½ in)

1 PR

2 PR

SKIRT FRONT 67 cm (26½ in)	SEAT 67 cm (26½ in)

68 cm (27 in)

3 PR

INSIDE BACK 71 cm (28 in)

82 cm (32 in)

4 PR

5 PR

5 x 68 cm = 3.4 m
(5 x 27 in = 135 in)

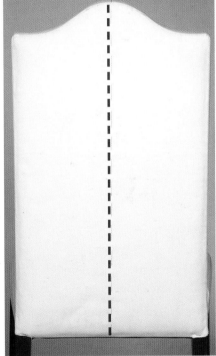

2 Mark the chair with a line of tacking stitches, the centre line of the inside and outside back and seat of the chair. Also mark the position of the top of the skirt.

3 Fold and mark with notches the centre line of the inside back, outside back and seat fabric pieces.

BACK LEG PLEAT 33 cm (13 in)	BACK LEG PLEAT 33 cm (13 in)	FRONT LEG PLEAT 23 cm (9 in)	FRONT LEG PLEAT 23 cm (9 in)

50 cm (20 in)

20 cm (8 in)

PIPING

70 cm (28 in)

4 Place the inside back and seat fabrics on the chair with right sides out. Pin to the centre line, and using pins, anchor the pieces in place all the way round the outside edges.

5 Fold the seat and back tuck-in allowances so that they are positioned flat against the inside back and seat.

7 Fold the inside back and seat tuck-ins together. Mark the point where the fabrics meet at the corners only.

8 Push a ruler into the chair to find the depth of the tuck-in. Add a 1.5 cm (⅝ in) seam allowance to this measurement and then cut away any excess tuck-in fabric.

6 Pin the back and seat corners to form darts.

9 Using a diagonal cut (from the inside to the outside), cut the tuck-in fabrics to the corner marks.

10 Push the tuck-in into the chair and position the inside back and seat fabrics together so that the two pieces meet in a neat diagonal seam at the sides. Position the seam carefully and pin in place. Trim away any excess fabric leaving a 1.5 cm (⅝ in) seam allowance.

11 Take the seat and inside back fabrics off the chair. Mark the position of the darts and side seams on the wrong side of the fabric. Re-pin the pieces with right sides together, using the markings as your guide. Machine stitch the darts.

12 Double stitch the marked corner seams to strengthen the seam. Also machine stitch the tuck-in pieces together. Cut away any excess fabric and neaten the seams using a zigzag or overlock stitch.

13 Re-fit the fabric to the inside back and seat, paying particular attention to the positioning of the fabric. Check the fit of the cover where the two pieces meet at the sides. Make any adjustments as required.

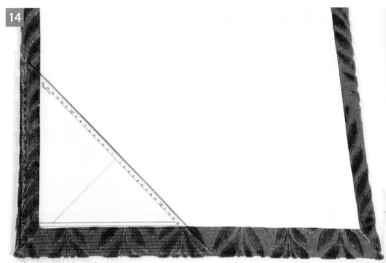

14 Make the three skirt panels:
• Attach the lining fabric to the hem of the skirt, leaving 8 cm (3 in) free at each end.
• Turn up the hem 5 cm (2 in) and turn the sides in 5 cm (2 in) and mitre the corners.
• Slip stitch the mitres and the lining fabric to the sides.

Note that the back edge of the skirt sides are wider at the bottom edge than the top to allow for the rake of the back legs.

15 Make the kick pleats:
• With right sides together, stitch the lining to the bottom edge of the fabric with a 1.5 cm (⅝ in) seam allowance.
• Turn the hem up 2.5 cm (1 in) and machine stitch the side seams.
• Turn through to the right sides and press in place.

Note that the back pleats are wider than the front to allow for the rake of the back legs.

16 Attach the lining fabric to the hem of the outside back fabric, turning the hem up 5 cm (2 in), and press in place. Mark the depth of the back skirt with a row of pins. Turn the sides in 5 cm (2 in) and quick mitre the corners. Slip stitch the mitres and the lining fabric to the sides. Herringbone stitch the top of the lining to the main fabric at the top of the back skirt.

19 Position and pin the skirt in place to the chair.

17 Measure the required depth of the skirt and kick pleats and add a 1.5 cm (⅝ in) seam allowance. Cut off any excess fabric above this point on each of the skirt and kick pleat pieces. Position the front and side skirt pieces and the contrast kick pleats together in sequence. The kick pleat should be 1 cm (⅜ in) shorter than the skirt pieces. Make sure the top of the pleats meet neatly and accurately. It may be necessary to tack the pleats to hold them in place.

18 Make and attach the contrast piping to the top edge of the skirt.

20 Pin the outside back panel to the back of the chair, lining up the back skirt with the side skirts.

21 Pin the front and back pieces together.

22 Mark the stitching line on both the back and front pieces of fabric. Mark or notch at appropriate places around the back and cut away any excess fabric, leaving a 1.5 cm (⅝ in) seam allowance.

23 Take the fabrics off the chair and stitch the piping to the inside back.

24 Stitch the skirt and pleat sections to the seat fabric, making a neat join where the back and skirt pieces meet. Cut the piping cord out of the piping fabric so that you can cross the two pieces of piping without causing excess bulk.

25 With right sides together, re-pin the back fabric to the inside back, matching any markings and notches, and machine stitch in place.

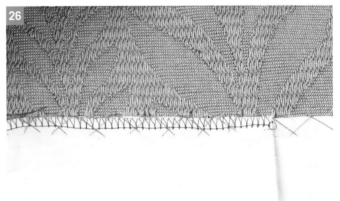

26 Herringbone stitch the top of the back kick pleats to the inside of the back fabric.

27 Neaten all the seams and raw edges with a zigzag or overlock stitch. Iron out any creases in the fabric and take out any temporary tacking stitches holding in the pleats. Fit and dress the loose cover on the chair.

GLOSSARY

Bondaweb: a very thin fusible interlining used for appliqué.

Calenderized: a finishing process for cloth. By passing the cloth through steam-heated rollers under pressure, glazed or watermark finishes are applied to fabric.

Double cloth: a type of fabric in which two or more sets of warps and one or more sets of weft threads are interconnected to form a two-layered cloth. Double-faced fabrics are a form of double cloth that has two right sides.

Dressing-in: the process of arranging the folds and drape of a curtain when it is first hung, or re-arranging the folds after the curtain has been opened and closed.

Embossing: a surface texture or pattern produced by passing the cloth under pressure and heat through engraved rollers.

End: an individual warp thread.

Feed dogs: feed the fabric through the sewing machine in the direction you are sewing.

Lambrequin: a traditionally-made pelmet with long sides.

Looper: the sewing machine's hook mechanism that catches the bottom thread when forming a stitch.

Mercerized: a caustic soda treatment on cotton yarn or thread to make it stronger and more lustrous.

Nap: the pile of the fabric that is brushed or raised, usually lying in one direction.

Pick: an individual weft thread.

Railroad: fabric where the pattern or stripe runs across the weft.

Room high: fabric that is made 2.85 to 3 m (9 ft 3 in to 9 ft 8 in) wide, thereby avoiding the need for seams. It is ideal for sheer and voile curtains.

Sanforize: a treatment for fabric to ensure that it will not shrink more than 1 per cent in washing.

Snatch-back: where the thread knots up under the fabric at the beginning of a machine stitch. To avoid this problem, hold the thread, or start with the needle down in the fabric as you begin to stitch.

Solprufe: a fabric treatment that gives protection from ultraviolet light.

Spring-back: the amount that curtains springs back when drawn together.

Tolerance: an amount of extra fabric required to allow for spring-back when curtains are drawn.

Vermicelli stitch: a meandering embroidery machine stitch where you drop the feed dogs so that the work can be moved freely in any direction.

Warp: the vertical thread running the length of the fabric.

Weft: the horizontal thread running across the width of the fabric.

Yoke: used on valances. It is the flat piece of fabric to which a pleated, gathered or shaped skirt is attached.

UK FIRE REGULATIONS

In the UK, loose covers for upholstered chairs must comply with the Furniture & Furnishings (Fire) (Safety) Regulations 1988. This means that loose covers for chairs made after 1st January 1950 must have fabrics that are fully compliant. Either:
• Inherent fire retardant
• Contain at least 75% of natural fibres: cotton, linen, silk, wool, viscose or modal, when it can be used together with a Schedule 3 Interliner/Barrier Cloth (Note: a fire retardant calico is not necessarily a barrier cloth under the terms of the regulations).
• Back-coated fire retardant.
    You cannot use an interliner/barrier cloth with fabrics containing more than 25% synthetic fibres i.e. acrylic and polyester.
    These notes are for guidance only. A guide to the UK Furniture & Furnishings (Fire) (Safety) Regulations can be downloaded from The Association of Master Upholsterers & Soft Furnishers' website: www.upholsterers.co.uk or the Furniture Industry Research Association's website: www.askfira.co.uk

RESOURCES AND ORGANIZATIONS

The Association of Master Upholsterers & Soft Furnishers
Unit Q1 Capital Point
Capital Business Park
Parkway
Trowbridge
Cardiff CF3 2PU
www.upholsterers.co.uk

FIRA International Ltd
www.askfira.co.uk

The Worshipful Company of Upholders
www.upholders.co.uk

FABRIC COMPANIES

Blendworth Fabrics
Crookley Park
Horndean PO8 0AD
www.blendworth.co.uk

Harlequin Fabrics
Ladybird House
Beeches Road
Loughborough LW11 2HA
www.harlequin.uk.com

Kobe (UK) Fabrics Ltd
Loddon Vale House
Hurricane Way
Woodley
Reading RG5 4UX
www.kobefab.com

LINING FABRICS

Edmund Bell
Belfry House
Roydsdale Way
Bradford BD4 6SU
www.edmundbell.co.uk

MATERIAL SUPPLIERS

Jaycotts
Unit D2
Chester Trade Park
Chester CH1 4LT
www.jaycotts.co.uk

Merrick & Day
Redbourne Hall
Redbourne
Gainsborough DN21 4JG
www.merrick-day.com

Price & Co
Regency House
North Street
Portslade BN41 1ES
www.price-regency.co.uk

Streets
Hurricane Way
Wickford Business Park
Wickford SS11 8YB
www.streets.co.uk

Whitemore & Thwaytes
Foxton House
Lowther Street
Penrith CA11 7UW
www.whitemoreandthwaytes.co.uk

QUILTING COMPANIES

Louis Moreau (The Quilters) Ltd
784–788 High Road
Tottenham
London N17 0DA
www.louismoreau.co.uk

SEWING MACHINES

Brother Sewing Machines
Shepley Street
Audenshaw
Manchester M34 5JD
www.brother.co.uk

TRACKS AND POLES

Cameron Fuller Ltd
Duchy Road
Heathpark
Honiton EX14 1YD
www.cameronfuller.co.uk

Integra Products Ltd
Eastern Avenue
Lichfield WS13 7SB
www.integra-products.co.uk

Silent Gliss Ltd
Pyramid Business Park
Poolhole Lane
Broadstairs CT10 2PT
www.silentgliss.co.uk

UPHOLSTERY MATERIALS

J A Milton Upholstery Supplies Ltd
Ellesmere Business Park
Ellesmere SY12 0EW
www.jamiltonupholstery.co.uk

FEATHER AND FOAM PADS

Aerofoam
30 Dalston Gardens
Stanmore HA7 1BY
+44 (0)20 8204 8411

ACKNOWLEDGEMENTS

In writing this book I would like to thank my family, friends, students and colleagues who have supported me throughout my career, particularly my tutors: Ernie Spratling, Malcolm Hopkins and Sue Clark, members of the Association of Master Upholsterers and Soft Furnishers and the Worshipful Company of Upholders.

My particular thanks and appreciation must go to Bertram Chapman MBE who has been my mentor, special advisor and great friend, whose support and enthusiasm have been a great source of inspiration to me.

I would also like to thank those people and organizations that have helped in the production of this book:

Tricia Butterworth for her help, enthusiasm and continued support
Ella Johnson for the use of her bedroom
Cathy Johnson and Sharon Brown of Stuft Interiors for their support
Corinne Masciocchi, editor
Edward Allwright, photographer
Harlequin Fabrics
Kobe UK Ltd
Blendworth Fabrics
Price & Co
Edmund Bells
Brother Sewing Machines

BIBLIOGRAPHY

The Encyclopaedia of Curtains, Catherine Merrick and Rebecca Day (Merrick & Day; 1999)

The Home Furnishings Workbook, Maureen Whitemore (Collins & Brown; 2002)

Complete Curtain-Making Course, Heather Luke (New Holland Publishers Ltd; 2007)

Tucks, Texture and Pleats, Jennie Rayment (JR Publications; 1994)

The Style Source Book, Judith Miller (Firefly Books; 2003)

The Illustrated Dictionary of Fabrics, Martin Hardingham (Book Club Associates; 1978)

Clothing Technology, Von Eberle (Verlag Europa-Lehrmittel; 2004)

A Comprehensive A–Z of Fabrics, Ann Ladbury (Magnum Books; 1981)

CONTACT THE AUTHOR

Wendy Shorter Interiors
www.wendyshorterinteriors.co.uk